CASESTUDIES

Super Sixes

The School Library and the Sixth Form

Edited by
Sally Dring

Series Editor
Geoff Dubber

Series Editor: Geoff Dubber

Acknowledgements

Sally Dring would like to thank all the contributors to this collection of case studies for their time, work and for answering all my queries with good humour, as well as the SLA's Publications Team of Geoff Dubber, Richard Leveridge and Jane Cooper, who work tirelessly to proof-read, edit and publish these publications.

Published by

School Library Association
1 Pine Court, Kembrey Park
Swindon SN2 8AD

Tel: 01793 530166 Fax: 01793 481182
E-mail: info@sla.org.uk
Web: www.sla.org.uk

Registered Charity Nos: 313660 and SC039453

© SLA 2016. All rights reserved.
ISBN: 978-1-903446-91-1

Printed by Holywell Press, Oxford

Contents

Introduction: Challenges and Opportunities   5
Sally Dring

Case Studies

Leading the Extended Project Qualification   8
John Iona

When Honesty Counts: Teaching academic writing style to Sixth Form International Baccalaureate Diploma Students at Box Hill School   16
Sarah Pavey

E-books and the E-library: Access at all times from anywhere!   23
Lucy Atherton

Read. Research. Revise! Moving to Higher Education: A Seamless Transition   33
Rosalind Buckland

Designing a Library Space for Sixth Form   40
Lesley Martin

Man Booker Prize Shadowing: Reigniting Reading for Pleasure by establishing a Sixth Form Book Club   45
James Curtis and Marissa Gisbourne

Contents

Working with Birmingham University in a Subject Context: Research Support for A Level History   52
Helen Emery

Cloud Computing: Using Google Apps   58
Darren Flynn, Andrew Walls and Caroline Shaw

Contributors   64

Please note:
The internet addresses (URLs) given in this book were correct at the time of going to press. However, due to the dynamic nature of the internet, web addresses and content may have changed or ceased to exist since publication. While we regret any inconvenience this may cause readers, no responsibility for any such changes can be accepted by the authors, editors or publisher.

Introduction

Challenges and Opportunities

Sally Dring

Learning Resources Manager, Literacy & Numeracy Coordinator, Ripon Grammar School. SLA Board member and Chair of Yorkshire & Humberside Branch

Working with Sixth Form students offers one of the biggest challenges, but also one of the biggest opportunities for school librarians. We can develop their information literacy skills to a much higher level to support A Level work and other qualifications; and we can delve into adult fiction to encourage reading for pleasure and all the stress-relieving delights that entails. It can be extremely rewarding observing our Sixth Formers blossoming and moving on to the next stage of their lives, whether that be into higher education or into the world of work.

Sixth Sense: The Sixth Form and the LRC, published in 2006, has been one of our most popular publications, and this is a new collection of up-to-date case studies from those currently working with 16 to 18-year-old students. In the ten years since the original publication appeared, there have been immense changes in the technology available for students, such as the advent of the widespread use of tablets in school, or BYOD (Bring Your Own Device) policies, not to mention the possibilities (and dangers) of social media. However, this means that the need for information literacy and research skills is even greater than before; information may be more accessible in greater quantity, but the ability to evaluate that information and select the best and most trustworthy for your task has not necessarily kept up with these changes. Contrary to the belief (by some) that all today's students are computer whizz-kids, anyone working in a school library knows that this is simply not true. They can find their way around, but information-seeking habits rarely go beyond Google and Wikipedia, and that includes for Sixth Formers too!

Universities, too, have reported that many of those arriving for their first year of study often lack the ability to learn and work independently, which includes proficiency in knowledge management. School librarians have the expertise to equip students with this knowledge and ease their transition into higher education. Indeed, many university websites now include a raft of information for Sixth Formers – good examples of this can be seen on the sites for the University of Cambridge[1] and UCL.[2] If we do our job well we can give our students a big advantage and reduce the stresses they will encounter as they move onto the next stage of their education. Working with our teaching colleagues to build these skills into subject learning is the ideal way to approach this task, although not always easy to do.

Academic honesty remains vital, and yet a recent study by *The Times* newspaper[3] found that around 45,000 university students have been caught cheating in the last three years. Interestingly, the method of plagiarising seems to have shifted from cut-and-paste (which is now easily detected by software such as Turnitin) towards purchasing ready-written essays or dissertations online. I know I've come across Sixth Form students who genuinely believe that this isn't cheating because the essay has been legitimately paid for (I don't think they've actually done it!). Imparting this basic understanding of academic honesty has to be one of the most important tasks for the school librarian working with those studying post-16.

Other areas currently being emphasised within schools are those of well-being, dealing with stress and developing empathy for others. A recent study by The Reading Agency[4] found that 'there is strong evidence that reading for pleasure can increase empathy, improve relationships with others, reduce the symptoms of depression and the risk of dementia, and improve wellbeing throughout life…' Sixth Form students today are under immense pressure and, understandably, this can mean that reading for pleasure takes a back seat for a while, even among keen readers. Maybe we can help in facilitating access to suitable literature and building in some time for this kind of activity, which in turn may help to reduce their feelings of stress. Similarly, the library as a space for working is constantly evolving with an emphasis on providing different areas for different ways of working, both individually and collaboratively.

Our thanks are due to the highly skilled and dedicated school librarians who have kindly agreed to share their expertise and experience work in a range of secondary schools in this publication. The wide ranging studies in this collection, demonstrate how school librarians can impart and develop the ever-important skills such as information literacy and understanding academic honesty, as well as methods of guiding students through the transition to Higher Education and targeting reading for pleasure with Sixth Formers. They will also take a look at issues which are newer, such as supporting qualifications like the EPQ (Extended Project Qualification), e-resources for post-GCSE library users and the advantages of cloud computing.

The library or LRC should be an integral part of our 16+ students' lives; it's just a matter of persuading them that our help and expertise *will* impact on their grades, just as surely as the information and knowledge gained from their teachers! I am reminded of the findings of the Erial Project from Illinois University which stated *'…the idea of a librarian as an academic expert who is available to talk about assignments and hold their hands through the research process is, in fact, foreign to most students. Those who even have the word "librarian" in their vocabularies often think library staff are only good for pointing to different sections of the stacks.'*[5] If university students feel like that now (as many certainly did five years ago) then our work with our Sixth Formers is of paramount importance! Read and enjoy.

References

[1] University of Cambridge, Information for Students: Study Skills. Available at: http://www.admin.cam.ac.uk/univ/plagiarism/students/skills/ (Accessed: 15 January 2016).

[2] UCL: Information for Current Students (Transition): Study Skills. Available at: https://www.ucl.ac.uk/transition/study-skills-resources (Accessed: 15 January 2016)

[3] The Times Education (2016), Universities face student cheating crisis, Available at: http://www.thetimes.co.uk/tto/education/article4654719.ece (Accessed: 15 January 2016)

[4] The Reading Agency (2015), Reading for pleasure builds empathy and improves well-being, research from The Reading Agency finds. Available at: http://readingagency.org.uk/news/media/reading-for-pleasure-builds-empathy-and-improves-wellbeing-research-from-the-reading-agency-finds.html (Accessed: 15 January 2016)

[5] Erial Project Illinois University (2011), What Students Don't Know, https://www.insidehighered.com/news/2011/08/22/erial_study_of_student_research_habits_at_illinois_university_libraries_reveals_alarmingly_poor_information_literacy_and_skills (Accessed 2 Feb. 2016)

Case Study 1

Leading the Extended Project Qualification

John Iona

Librarian and Information Manager, Oasis Academy, Enfield
Joint winner of the SLA School Librarian of the Year Award 2013

What is the EPQ?

Project qualifications are offered at three different levels through AQA, OCR and EDEXCEL. Level 1 is a pre-GCSE qualification (called the Foundation Project Qualification or FPQ), Level 2 a GCSE level qualification (Higher Project Qualification or HPQ[6]), and Level 3 (Extended Project Qualification or EPQ) is an A2-level qualification. For the Sixth Form students in your school, taking this course will come with the award of valuable UCAS points as follows:

Grade	UCAS Points
A*	70
A	60
B	50
C	40
D	30
E	20

Source: http://www.aqa.org.uk/subjects/projects/aqa-certificate/EPQ-7993/why-choose/performance-tables

For your school, each grade will also contribute to performance points, and these can also be found on the AQA website at the URL above.

For the purpose of this case study, I will focus on the Level 3 qualification and the AQA specification.

Background

My experience of delivering project qualifications began in 2011, when I was asked to run the level two qualification with a group of ten Year 11 students. I ran the course using the EDEXCEL exam board, and managed to secure seven pass grades at C and above.

The following year (2012–13), I ran the course for a larger cohort (approximately 40) of Level 2 students, but also the AQA Level 3 course was offered to our first group of Year 12 students. While running the level two course, I was able to support and work with the teacher who was responsible for the Level 3, helping to plan and deliver sessions, support the students on the course and eventually mark the ten projects from this particular group at the end of the year.

Finally, in 2013–14, I was asked to run both courses. This involved 18 Year 11 students on the Level 2, and 19 Year 13 students taking the Level 3 course.

What does it involve?

At each level and specification the project involves students setting themselves a project task, idea or question along with project objectives. This is usually formed after some preliminary ideas-generation and research to come up with initial ideas, which are discussed with their Supervisor and then either approved, or adapted to be approved. With the AQA specification, at all three levels, there is a 'Production Log' that students and their Supervisor complete over the course of the project. This document guides, structures and evidences the process.

Students' final project outcomes can range from a 5,000-word essay or report, to a more practical outcome such as an experiment, an object or artefact, or a performance. If the project involves a practical outcome of some kind, this must be accompanied by a research-based write-up of approximately 1,000 words.

Choice of titles and projects should be related to the individuals' own areas of interest, perhaps to a subject they are currently studying in their A-levels or perhaps to the course they are hoping to begin at university. In this sense, it is good practice to encourage students to choose a project that will take their current learning further and be something that will show engagement in an area that they have a passion for, as this will prove valuable to refer to in personal statements on UCAS applications, university interviews or job applications. Some examples of chosen EPQ titles include:

- To what extent would the UK's economy be damaged by leaving the EU?
- Should the death penalty be brought back to the UK?
- Is marriage irrelevant in modern society?
- Climate change: Are we doing enough?

Once students have their proposed title and objectives approved they can begin further in-depth research to allow them to carry out their project by developing and informing their ideas, and/or answer their question. During the research process there are a number of milestones, set out and recorded in the Production Log, for points of reflection and discussion with the Supervisor on how the project is developing.

Once the student has completed their research and are in a position to move forward, they can move towards the main outcome, be it the report/essay or putting together the practical outcome along with the write-up.

On completion of the project, with the AQA syllabus, students are required to put together a presentation about their project to an audience. This forms part of the assessment and is a chance for students to present their findings, and tell the story of their project in an evaluative and reflective way.

Delivering the course

With the cohort of 19 Year 13 pupils I had a weekly, timetabled double-lesson (100 minutes) with the group. The students were selected for the course on the basis that they had dropped one or more courses, either AS-level or BTEC qualification, studied in Year 12 and needed a new course to study alongside their remaining A2s or BTECs. The EPQ was chosen for these students as a course that would provide them with an opportunity to secure valuable UCAS points for their university applications, as well as being a good introduction to what to expect with undergraduate study.

During the scheduled lessons, I used the time to deliver the taught element required by the specification, which is expected to be 30 guided learning hours, as well as to meet with the students individually to guide their project work. The course specification recommends that the project will incorporate 120 guided learning hours from students and these timetabled lessons form part of this total, with the remaining hours consisting of students' guided, but independent, work on their projects.

The timetabled lessons were an opportunity to teach pupils the skills that they would require for carrying out their project appropriately, preparing them at each stage of the process. Having an understanding of what pupils are being assessed on, the Assessment Objectives (AOs) and marking criteria, as well as what an A-grade, C-grade and E-grade project looks like are very important for planning valuable taught sessions. I used the AOs to understand what skills and competencies students were expected to evidence within their projects, so that I could plan sessions that would give them the necessary skills. The breakdown and short description of the AOs are as follows:

	Assessment Objectives (AOs)	Weighting
AO1	**Manage** Identify, design, plan, and carry out a project, applying a range of skills, strategies and methods to achieve objectives.	20%
AO2	**Use Resources** Research, critically select, organise and use information, and select and use a range of resources. Analyse data apply relevantly and demonstrate understanding of any links, connections and complexities of the topic.	20%
AO3	**Develop and Realise** Select and use a range of skills, including, where appropriate, new technologies and problem-solving, to take decisions critically and achieve planned outcomes.	40%
AO4	**Review** Evaluate all aspects of the extended project, including outcomes in relation to stated objectives and own learning and performance. Select and use a range of communication skills and media to present evidenced project outcomes and conclusions in an appropriate format.	20%

Source: AQA (2015) Level 3 Extended Project Qualification (7993) Specification. P.8. Online. Available at: http://www.aqa.org.uk/subjects/projects/aqa-certificate/EPQ-7993 or direct link http://filestore.aqa.org.uk/subjects/AQA-W-7993-SP-15.PDF

These AOs are then broken down further into level descriptors for the purposes of assessment and marking, with each AO having three bands of marks to be awarded for the student's level of achievement.

When it comes to planning lessons then, it was important to give students the opportunity to learn how to both carry out, and evidence appropriately, the range of skills identified in the marking criteria. The initial sessions were based on planning, and incorporated activities devoted to:

- Identifying potential topics from interest areas
- Creating detailed mind-maps that evidence careful thought, pupils' current ideas and knowledge, key questions and topics, and the potential areas for research
- Finding sources for carrying out initial research – what various, available sources are suitable in these early stages?
- Forming an appropriate research question, that allows for in-depth research and engagement with a topic
- Project planning and GANTT charts[7]
- Planning and managing time through the course.

These lessons introduced the course, and time was also devoted to looking at examples of projects, forming and sharing ideas in groups, and using an example topic as a class to model these initial planning activities.

Once all pupils had their initial project titles and outcomes approved, I moved on to lessons that focussed on the research element in more detail. These sessions included:

- Planning research, identifying and using key-words and potential sources, using the initial mind-maps to guide the process
- Using the Library (both school and external Libraries) resources available, including books, journals and accessing and using relevant databases etc.
- Being a critical researcher, evaluating sources and their reliability
- Using different methods to record research and source information (e.g. bibliographic details).

The research stage of the project and course is, in many ways, the trickiest to manage for both the teacher/supervisor and the student. It can be the loosest part of the course as it relies on students mostly working independently on their projects, finding, reading and learning from their research, and letting it guide their work. For students this is an unfamiliar way of working and so they can become unfocussed and find it difficult to manage. For the teacher it can be tricky to monitor and requires clear milestones to be set so that students have particular pieces of work to either submit, discuss or present, to guide their time and their work.

The next set of lessons concern the task of writing up the final essay, or report. Once students finish their research and have reached a point at which they are in a position to begin answering their project title question, the taught element needs to address report-writing skills. During these lessons, students were taught the following:

- Planning and structuring an academic report – looking at different forms, styles and structures of academic writing to suit the purpose and topic of the report
- How to use research both to plan, and in, a report
- Plagiarism, using quotations and referencing
- Creating an annotated bibliography.

All of my students carried out projects that required a written essay/report, and so writing a 5,000 word essay took many students far beyond their comfort zone. They required a lot of dedicated support during this time to help them structure and break down this piece of extended writing, and for some students it was not until this point that they realised that they did not carry out enough research to give them the required knowledge to answer their questions in the depth necessary for a piece of writing on this scale. Those students that did not plan effectively or work hard enough to complete the various activities and meet the necessary milestones during the planning and research stages, found that they were not able to meet the demands of writing the essay and so some students, at this stage, felt that they could not complete the course. For me, I learned that I needed to be stricter with the earlier deadlines and demand more rigorous work to be evidenced and submitted at previous milestones, so that I could ensure that students were progressing at the required level with their projects, to set them up appropriately for these final stages.

Once the reports have been written and submitted, the final stage of the course is the review element which involves a written evaluation in the Production Log, as well as the presentation discussed above. During this stage of the course, lessons focussed on:

- Reflective writing
- Self-evaluation
- Planning a presentation
- Public speaking.

These lessons covered the necessary skills for pupils to complete these final assessed pieces of work.

Many of the skills covered above at Level 3 are reflected in, and transferable down to, Level 2 and across the two exam boards. So through the management and delivery of this course I found that most of the lessons and materials I had planned and used with the EDEXCEL Level 2 cohort, could be easily adapted and differentiated up to meet the demands of the AQA EPQ.

Ways to get involved

There are a range of ways that librarians can get involved with EPQ in their schools. As you can see from the information above, much of what we do as librarians in terms of information literacy falls within the bounds of the EPQ, and the very nature of the course lends itself to the involvement of the library and librarian in various forms. The skills that are necessary for students to master in order to excel in the course are clearly linked to undergraduate study, and form part of a transferable repertoire for any Sixth Form student to acquire. With the guidance and input of the librarian, the research and information specialist in the school, on the teaching and delivery of course content, there can only be further positive impact on the quality of the course as a whole and better grade outcomes as a result.

While managing and delivering the course may go beyond what many would consider undertaking, depending on the way the course is structured and administered in each context may provide opportunities for librarians to lend their expertise. Librarians could consider being a Supervisor, and guiding one or a small group of students through their projects. School librarians should also consider offering to be part of planning the taught element, perhaps taking responsibility for planning and delivering particular sessions or at least having an input into them and helping to produce materials to support this. Other ways of supporting the course may be to offer drop-in sessions for EPQ students, to offer support on particular areas such as using library databases, or how to write a bibliography, or one-to-one research interviews where a student can discuss their project and the librarian can offer tailored advice to them. Finally, delivering research guides, crib-sheets, VLE pages, dedicated to EPQ students bringing together specific resources or advice on particular elements of the course could also be a valuable source for both students and teachers involved in the course.

In conclusion

The EPQ course has been a fantastic way to develop my status with Sixth Form students, and staff, and for these students to see the relevance and importance of wider research using the Library. From my own professional development perspective, it has allowed me to gain a real insight into how to structure and deliver a course from start to finish, as well as the process of planning lessons and activities that integrate information and literacy while fitting into the broader context of a qualification.

Editor's note: John has also very kindly shared much of his EPQ material on the Learning and Teaching section of the SLA website – details can be found at http://www.sla.org.uk/learning-and-teaching.php. There is also some valuable EPQ material shared on this same site by ex-SLA Board member Carolyn Copland.

The SLA offers its own online Extended Project Qualification (EPQ) training programme: http://www.sla.org.uk/cpd-epq.php

References

[6] If you're interested in becoming involved in HPQ work do look at the SLA Voices publication *Taking a Leading Role: HPQ Level 2 and the School Librarian* by Barbara Band (2012).

[7] If you're unfamiliar with GANTT charts do take a look at http://www.gantt.com/

Case Study 2

When Honesty Counts: Teaching Academic Writing Style to Sixth Form International Baccalaureate Diploma Students at Box Hill School

Sarah Pavey MSc FCLIP
Independent consultant and trainer, previously librarian at Box Hill School, Surrey

The exponential growth of information available at the touch of a button over the last few decades has resulted in Higher Education establishments placing great importance on the correct attribution of sources within any written assignment. Yet a report by DEMOS, *Truth, Lies and the Internet*,[8] concludes that students find evaluation of resources they find to back up their claims difficult to say the least. In order for students to be successful at university it is important that we teach them these skills so they can master their first undergraduate year without too much pain, and we can mediate the shock of academic writing style. With this in mind it was decided to run a series of talks, workshops and surgeries for the Sixth Form at Box Hill School as a collaborative project between the Librarian and the International Baccalaureate Diploma Co-ordinator. However, this was not without challenges as will be described in this case study.

Background

The students in the Sixth Form at Box Hill School are drawn from diverse backgrounds. The introduction of the International Baccalaureate Diploma Programme[9] as the sole qualification offered in Years 12 and 13 in 2009 resulted in a sizeable number of Year 11 leavers deciding to pursue A Levels elsewhere. As a result the Sixth Form intake comprised mostly of students from overseas and other local schools. Although A Levels were re-introduced in 2013 the percentage of new students is still relatively high. This impacts on the teaching of information literacy skills since it cannot be assumed all students have reached the same level of proficiency.

The International Baccalaureate Diploma contains a compulsory Extended Essay element and a Theory of Knowledge Essay (both of which must be passed at a minimum of Grade D) plus various Internal Assessments for the six subjects chosen. All of these elements require an academic style and marks are awarded for correct referencing. So for these students it is imperative that they master academic honesty processes if they are to gain the grades they need for university or even just to pass the Diploma.

The Sixth Form at Box Hill School, as a co-educational independent boarding school, attracts many overseas students, mostly from Germany and Eastern Europe but also some from Asia. Some choose to study for the IB Diploma in English so that they can gain a dual language award. Although a proportion of these students will have spent a year in the International Study Centre at the School to try and raise their level of written English, not all take this route and so some work is submitted in their native language which makes teaching academic honesty that bit more interesting!

So taking into account all of these challenges we devised a mix of deliveries with the support of the teaching staff.

The teaching programme

It would have been impossible to deliver what was needed in just one short lecture. We had found from work with Year 10s in the school that information skills were more likely to be retained if they were delivered at the point of need and then reinforced on a regular basis and we decided to take a similar approach with the Sixth Form since the big essay assignments did not kick in until late in the Spring Term of Year 12.

A. Collaborative Teaching

The successful approach of planning projects jointly that I had implemented for younger year groups was continued for the Sixth Form. Here the subject teacher and I, as Librarian, would draw up a mark scheme for assessment. While the teacher awarded points for subject content and understanding, I gave points for evidence of good research practice, academic honesty and referencing and presentation. Because we wanted to emphasise the importance of academic style to the students, I was responsible for half the total marks in many cases.

Of course in order to achieve this, it was important first to show the students what they needed to do. This induction took place in the classroom when the topic for research was first introduced. The teacher explained the task and the mark scheme and then handed over to me. I brought a box of books on the topic and then showed the students the online catalogue with the virtual topic box which, in addition to the book titles, had downloadable booklets offering advice on referencing and write up and also suggested databases and mobile apps. The books were then distributed to the class and, in pairs, students fed back to the group whether they felt the resource would be useful in the context of the project. Using examples of the most popular books I would then show how to write a reference in an accepted style using the citation generator in our Library Management System, Access-It, or using an app such as EasyBib or QuickCite. We also covered reference making via the Word referencing tab.

Some lower ability students found the construction of references confusing and so I devised a series of A4 cards each with one part of a reference. Groups of six students were given a set of cards and a type of resource eg a website, a book, a journal. Between themselves, they sorted out which cards they would use to enable someone else to locate the information and then they lined up in front of their peers in the correct order. The rest of the class could suggest amendments or rearrange the card holders. For any element written in italics the card holder had to lean over. This provided a memorable game and proved more successful in retention of the information due to the kinaesthetic element.

Once the class had mastered the construction process we were able to reinforce what had been learned using some guessing games that I made available online.[10] This enabled students to continue self-learning outside lessons.

Because the collaborative classroom sessions had to focus on a specific topic, there was not time to cover more than methods of research and the presentation of the end product to include a bibliography and in text citation. However, the ability to write a reference is very different to knowing when something needs to be referenced in the first place, and it was decided that a series of more dedicated teaching sessions was needed to convey this part of the process.

B. Assemblies and Tutor Time sessions

The Sixth Form at Box Hill School had separate assemblies on occasions and with the IB Co-ordinator and Head of Sixth Form we decided to run two sessions – avoiding plagiarism and essay construction using mind mapping. A half hour slot was dedicated to each topic held two weeks apart. Because the time was short a game based approach was adopted to explain plagiarism. This exercise 'Jail or Freedom'[11] was also made available on the internet so that students could revisit the examples. I emphasised that referencing is there to authenticate their work which is so important when the amount of information available is so vast. I underpinned the message using real life examples of plagiarism and the effect this has on other people not just the originator of the idea that has been stolen and asked them to question what will happen in the future if information cannot be trusted. I also showed them the sanctions they could expect should they plagiarise work culminating in not being allowed to take public examinations.[12] Because the Sixth Form Tutors were also present it served as an INSET to make these teachers aware of what is and what is not acceptable practice.

The mind mapping write up was shown as a brief MS Powerpoint[13] but was then backed up with an hour long lesson on the essay writing process during tutor periods. Tutor groups were combined so that delivery for everyone was within a month.

The lesson was designed to show how to write up information from sources using your own words. The class was introduced to the idea of writing an essay on extraterrestrial life. First they were shown a chart containing data of UFO sightings with no further explanation. After two minutes the slide was taken away and the students were asked to write a heading: 'where is the best place to spot a UFO?' and then to write underneath what they recalled from the chart. Of course those who had made notes found this easier. We then constructed a reference because although it was paraphrased the information was still based on someone else's idea. The exercise was then repeated but using video information and a heading 'How likely is it that extraterrestrials exist?'. It was surprising how many students did not take notes while watching the video, despite the previous test, and did not realise this too needed a reference. In the final part of the lesson, the students had to insert a quote into each of their paragraphs. They were given a choice of three – all designed to deceive and which highlighted the need to check the authenticity of resources at a deeper level.

Again this active learning approach proved successful with this age group and by selecting mostly visual information for the exercises even those students with less fluency in English could relate to the concepts.

C. Individual surgery appointments

Because the Extended Essay and Theory of Knowledge Essay are an obligatory part of the International Baccalaureate Diploma Programme, students need to pass these elements with at least a Grade D. Heavy emphasis is placed upon academic honesty and referencing according to academic style by the IBO.[14] So, at Box Hill School, the Librarian was expected to work with students to make sure they have the best possible chance of success. By not becoming a supervisor, the Librarian could freely give time to individuals who may need further guidance and hand holding.

Box Hill School has two weeks in the year when students in the Lower School attend expeditions and are off site. For Year 12 this time has now been given over to preparation for their written assignments and essays. In addition for those struggling to meet deadlines I ran an activity club offering my help on Wednesday afternoons. The idea was to set up surgery appointments which students could sign up to individually or they could bring a friend. At the end of the session I would write them a prescription of what they needed to do next to perfect their essay.

The surgeries usually entailed reading through the essay with the student and identifying any places that needed an additional reference or where a more authoritative source was required. Due to language barriers this sometimes involved the student translating and then reading the essay aloud. With an essay of 4000 words we sometimes had to work in stages but it enabled me to pick up a smattering of Japanese, Farsi, Italian and German! Once this was complete we would then check the formatting together and ensure that, if the essay was in a foreign language, the style was acceptable to that country. This was important because the person marking the text would be a native speaker.

D. Plagiarism check with Turnitin

Once the essays were at a final draft stage I passed them through our subscription plagiarism checker Turnitin.[15] This product was chosen because it is the system favoured by examinations boards, universities and the IBO. However, we do not use it to catch students out but as an educational tool to help write to an academically acceptable standard. We could allow self-checking but for the pedagogical aspect it is more pertinent to discuss the report with the individual student. I do not exclude quotes, small matches or references so that we can see what is correct as well as what might need tweaking. This means that a humanities student who may include a lot of quoted material might score as high as 60% whereas a science student with much personal experimental date could score 10% or less. It is not helpful for these students to compare results without explanation. The reports are colour coded and so it is also useful to point out to students that there should be plenty of coloured passages in their introduction but that their conclusion should be plain because it is in their own words with their own thoughts and recommendations.

Evidence and conclusions

So was this time consuming process worth the investment? Well the evidence would suggest yes. I initiated the programme when I first arrived at Box Hill School to set up the IB Library. Enthusiasm for the qualification was at a high and so the quality of support was given greatest priority. The grades were good and the first cohort of students all passed the essay elements of the course and achieved their

Diplomas. However after two years the IB Co-ordinator changed and my involvement diminished. The grades dipped and some students failed. My part was reinstated and then developed and the level of passes increased to the extent that in 2014 all students exceeded the minimum pass and collected at least one extra point towards their Diploma total. This meant some were able to attend their chosen university despite not quite achieving the subject grade demanded in their offer.

But this investment has far greater long term benefits. When the drop out figures for first year undergraduates are considered, those students completing the IB Diploma rather than A levels are more likely to complete their degree.[16] This has to be in part due to the nature of the academic style that is taught for this qualification and their understanding of academic honesty as part of that process. Universities expect students to conform to this and there are harsh sanctions for those that do not. For A level students where this has not been underpinned as part of their studies, there is a temptation not to take it seriously enough and then to receive an unwelcome shock after the submission of their first piece of work. It is a steep learning curve for these students. The gratifying element for me, is when students returned to Box Hill School and thanked me personally for making their life at university so much easier. One in particular told me he still used the referencing booklet and web presentation I made for his final dissertation and that he hoped I did not mind but he has passed it on to some other final year undergraduates.

The importance of academic honesty cannot be underestimated and if we are to continue 'standing on the shoulders of giants' to further our understanding of the world we need to ensure that we base our theories on firm foundations and authoritative sources of information not just the Google/Wikipedia culture. In the Sixth Form we can appeal to this sense of social responsibility even if they are not studying for a qualification with an extended written element. It is worth claiming some time from their busy schedule to underpin concepts of academic honesty through games and examples. You might be interested to delve into this at a deeper level and undertake the School Library Association's Online Course on Academic Honesty.[17] This will enable you to access games that could form part of a teaching programme.

References

8 Bartlett, C. and Miller, J. *Truth Lies and the Internet: A Report into Young People's Digital Fluency.* Available at: http://www.demos.co.uk/publications/truth-lies-and-the-internet 2011

9 IBO *International Baccalaureate Diploma Programme.* Available at: http://www.ibo.org/en/programmes/diploma-programme/ 2015

10 Pavey, S. *Referencing and Bibliographies Harvard (Author Date).* Available at: http://www.authorstream.com/Presentation/SarahPavey-352849-referencing-using-harvard-citation-education-ppt-powerpoint/ 2010

11 Pavey, S. *Plagiarism Game: Jail or Freedom.* Available at: http://www.authorstream.com/Presentation/SarahPavey-1081155-plagiarism-game-updated/ 2011

12 JCQ *Plagiarism in Examinations.* Available at: http://www.jcq.org.uk/exams-office/malpractice/plagiarism-in-examinations 2015

13 Pavey, S. *Essay Writing Mind Map.* Available at: http://www.authorstream.com/Presentation/SarahPavey-1365094-powerpoint-essay-writing-mind-map/ 2012

14 Garza, C. *Academic Honesty Principles to Practice.* Available at: http://www.ibo.org/contentassets/71f2f66b529f48a8a61223070887373a/academic-honesty.-principles-into-practice—-celina-garza.pdf 2014

15 Turnitin. *Turnitin Home Page.* Available at: http://turnitin.com/ 2015

16 HESA *International Baccalaureate Students studying at UK Higher Education Institutions: How do they fare?* Available at http://static1.squarespace.com/static/50c2031de4b02a7395e3e36f/t/51190655e4b085e20f826d7e/1360594517063/HESAUKPostsec_Final_Report.pdf 2011

17 Pavey, S. *Academic Honesty Training.* Available at: http://www.sla.org.uk/academic-honesty-training.php 2015

Case Study 3

E-books and the e-library: Access at all times from anywhere

Lucy Atherton

Wellington College – The Mallinson Library

Wellington College is a co-ed independent school in Berkshire with around 1,050 students from 13–18. It is predominantly boarding but has a number of day students. The library was re-developed in 2012 to create a flexible and attractive space for students. A blend of hard copy and e-books, print magazines, online resources, large touch-screen computers and iPads are provided to encourage collaborative learning and to remove all barriers to our library services. The library has a vibrant atmosphere with glass pods of varying sizes to facilitate group work, social learning or individual study. There is also a designated silent study room for individuals to focus without distraction. The school has a CYOD (Choose Your Own Device) policy which frees up space and eliminates the need for cumbersome desktop computers. Fast Wi-Fi is provided throughout the school.

There is a large Sixth Form of 470 students and from this year's issue statistics it is clear that Y12 and Y13 are the biggest borrowers of Library stock. Both A level and the IB Diploma (International Baccalaureate) courses are offered. Since its implementation in 2008 the IB DP has become increasingly popular. It is pleasing to see that the IBO insists upon the presence of a professional librarian to support the qualification and recognises the importance, indeed the essential nature of a school library. The Extended Essay is a key part of the Diploma and an area where the library and librarians play an important role in supporting independent learning and research.

Super Sixes

e-Library – Access to e-resources at all times from anywhere!

What we offer

Over the last few years we have developed a collection of authoritative subscription-based online resources which make up the Wellington College e-Library along with reliable and content-rich free websites such as TEDTalks (https://www.ted.com/talks), Khan Academy (https://www.khanacademy.org/), Cambridge School Shakespeare (http://www.cambridgeschoolshakespeare.com/), RSC Learn Chemistry (http://www.rsc.org/Learn-Chemistry) and Stanford Encyclopedia of Philosophy (http://plato.stanford.edu/).

The e-Library is currently hosted on our Firefly Intranet although we are moving over to use Office 365 and Sharepoint. I designed the e-Library interface to be attractive and colourful so the icons look like apps rather than a series of wordy links. This is not a static collection and we are constantly canvassing pupils and staff for feedback on how useful they find it. We are not afraid to drop a resource if it is under-used or if a more relevant one becomes available. The majority of online resources offer access to usage statistics so that impact and value for money can be assessed.

It is exciting to be able to offer Sixth Formers the opportunity to access these academic resources at all times. We know from the email enquiries to the library during holidays that pupils are making use of JSTOR, Questia, Cambridge Companions and the library catalogue out of school.

Library Catalogue – integrating e-book records

The Access-IT library catalogue (http://library.accessitsoftware.com/) is available via the e-Library so students can see our Library holdings. A 'Reading Lists' feature enables them to view each academic department's 'Top Ten Reads' and see immediately which ones are available. These books are subject based and graduated so that the final book is the most challenging. The idea is for Sixth Formers to read all the books in the subject they intend to study at university. The catalogue also contains records for the e-book versions.

An exciting development in our Access-IT Library Management System is 'One Search' which provides the opportunity to search external content alongside the catalogue holdings. Online resources to be included are selected by the Librarian (eg. a range of the e-Library resources) which enables students to search the catalogue and this content simultaneously.

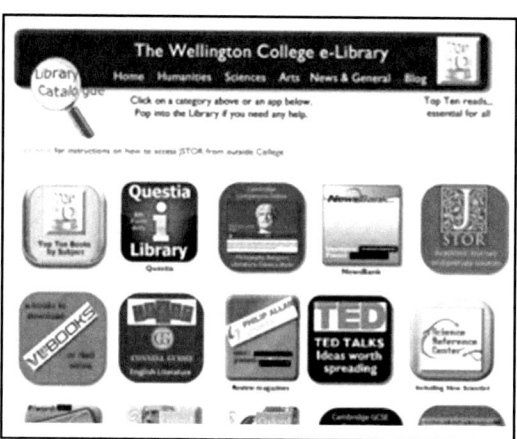

Screen shot of Wellington College e-Library

Removing barriers to access to information

I am keen to remove barriers to our online resources as I am all too aware that pupils immediately turn to Google or Wikipedia when embarking on research. Where possible we try to avoid any additional need to log into the resources. Pupils and staff need to log on to the Intranet to access the e-resources but once on the school network the majority of the databases permit access via IP address recognition, thus negating the need to log on a second time. Shibboleth and Athens provide a single sign-on alternative (as used by universities to access their e-resources) but there are additional costs and IT support time.

A look at some of the key subscription-based online resources on the e-Library

Questia School from Cengage Learning

This vast resource is available for all Sixth Form students. Questia School (https://www.questiaschool.com) consists of e-books, academic articles, newspaper and magazine articles. We demonstrate it to all IB students and recommend it as a starting point for the Extended Essay research. Invariably they will find books and scholarly articles on any subject they can think of and, as each Sixth Form student has an individual account, they can save searches in named projects and bookmark and annotate pages. The database is so immense that students have to learn how to refine their search terms and we assist them in developing their search skills.

JSTOR

Demand for JSTOR (http://www.jstor.org) from staff and Sixth Form was high so we committed to unlimited user access despite the expense. It is worth noting that JSTOR, as with a large number of key e-resources,

can be bought as part of a consortium of schools which considerably reduces the cost to individual schools. It is available via IP recognition so that one click from the e-Library provides pupils with a wealth of scholarly articles ideally suited to their Sixth Form extended written projects as well as coursework and essays. This has been an exciting addition to our e-Library and is a valuable step in the preparation of our students for study in Higher Education. JSTOR has recently been developing its services to secondary schools and I am testing out their 'Research Basics' online course with a view to using it with our pupils. It is a series of video lessons on research and citation skills, followed up with quizzes checking understanding of the concepts and online badges.

Connell Guides – great mix of print and online content

Connell Guides (http://connellguides.com) are a series of pocket-size, succinct insights into the classic works of English Literature. They are attractive and engagingly written giving a range of expert views on key works of literature. With our subscription we receive six new books each year. This also entitles us to access useful online content including short guides to modern texts, produced every two months and available to download as mobi, pdf or epub files. They also produce critical essays, fortnightly reviews, videos of experts talking about individual texts, and literature quizzes. The content is continuously expanding so there is always new material to enhance students' knowledge.

Exploiting online resources – current awareness bulletin

I noticed that the daily print newspapers on display in the Library foyer were under-used. Pressures of life in a busy boarding school meant that the pupils sometimes lack the time to read. I decided to develop a library-produced weekly News Digest using the printed newspapers and also *The Times* articles from our NewsBank (http://www.newsbank.com) database (as *The Times* now charges a subscription for online access). The Library staff scan the papers on a daily basis for key articles relating to curriculum subjects and other areas of interest to the school community such as Medicine, Veterinary Medicine, Service, Expeditions, Society and Diversity and the Environment. We send out an email to all staff and students containing the links to these articles online, all grouped by subject or theme. So, for example a prospective Law student can quickly keep up with developments in the legal world or a future Medic can read more deeply around her subject. It is also a valuable way of highlighting new e-resources and content. During Library induction sessions we promote the News Digest to Sixth Formers motivating them by citing the example of a girl who last year received her place to study Medicine at Oxford and cheerfully informed me that an article we'd provided in our bulletin helped her with an interview question.

What we do
A level students EPQ (Extended Project Qualification)

All A level students receive introductory demonstrations to researching using the e-Library through a course in Project and Research Skills hosted in the library pods. This is led by teachers but the professional librarians give demonstrations of the e-Library and explain how the librarians can support the EPQ with inter-library loans of books and articles from the London and British Libraries, and assist with referencing and the initial research.

Supporting the IB Extended Essay (EE) – A three-pronged approach

1. Whole group talk

I give an introductory talk to all the Lower Sixth pupils studying IB as they embark on their EE research. This gives them an introduction to how the Library can support them with obtaining articles and books, assistance with referencing and bibliographies, a reminder of the importance of avoiding plagiarism and a brief overview of the huge array of online resources available to them. Once the supervisors are assigned and the broad theme of the essay decided upon, we run more in-depth sessions for all the IB students in a carousel.

2. Subject-based sessions

For the larger subjects, for example, there may be 20 students writing a History Extended Essay. We run workshops going into greater detail about the online resources such as NewsVault (http://gale.cengage.co.uk/product-highlights/general-reference/gale-historical-newspapers/gale-newsvault.aspx), an extensive collection of newspapers going back to the 17th Century. In this more targeted way we can fully explain the features of this valuable resource. We also show students how to access the London Library (http://www.londonlibrary.co.uk) catalogue for additional material and look at *History Today* (http://www.historytoday.com) magazine online archive, JSTOR, Active History (http://www.activehistory.co.uk) and Rudbeck IB History Revision website (https://rudbeck-ib-history-revision.wikispaces.com).

3. One to one informal interviews

Following on from the above we have a list of students and their essay topics and aim to see all of them individually to discuss any additional research assistance they need and offer advice about how to tackle the planning.

Lessons learnt in setting up an e-Library:

- Continuous evaluation is essential – invite feedback
- Talk about and demonstrate the e-Library at every opportunity
- Remind teaching staff at frequent intervals – Head of Department meetings, invite academic departments to hold meetings in the library and demonstrate e-resources
- Be proactive – visit classrooms to talk about subject specific e-resources
- 'Show and tell' e-Library at Professional Learning (CPD) events and encourage use of the library for these events
- Promote new resources through emails, 'app of the week', weekly emailed News Digest, posters on the backs of toilet doors!
- Talk to other school librarians – swap opinions about resources and find out about new ones
- Online resources come and go – sometimes great content is limited by poor access, an un-helpful interface or disappointing search features.

E-books

We decided to introduce e-books at the same time as the Library was re-developed. Three years on the e-book situation is still complex and there is no one-size fits all solution. This was the early days of e-book platforms and we were the first school to subscribe to VLeBooks, the e-book platform from Browns Books for Students (http://www.brownsbfs.co.uk/pages/VLeBooks). E-book content on the portal has vastly increased since then and we can now find an e-book, order it and make it available to a pupil in a matter of minutes. In general, pupils don't ask for an e-book and invariably prefer to go away with a printed book in their hands but if a holiday is coming up e-versions can be incredibly useful. For example I was asked by a pupil for books on the physics of golf for her EPQ. She had been unable to find what she needed in our printed stock so I searched VLeBooks – ordered two books, they arrived five minutes later and she could make use them over the

Easter holiday wherever she was in the world via the free VLeBooks app on her android or Apple device (including iPhones, iPads, tablets). The books can also be read online anywhere that has Internet or Wi-Fi access or on a desktop or laptop PC using Adobe Digital Editions software (http://www.adobe.com/uk/products/digital-editions.html).

Screen shot of the VLeBooks web interface. 335,000+ e-books, integrated dictionary, create and share notes, customisable homepage (www.brownsbfs.co.uk/pages/VLeBooks)

One of the deciding factors when choosing VLeBooks was the ability to permit multiple concurrent users. Whether this is possible or not is stipulated by the publisher. Therefore quite a large number of fiction titles can only be read by a single user at any given time. However, for many non-fiction titles we opt for the credits option which enables a whole class to read the same book concurrently.

Library Lists feature

The e-book platform is being improved all the time and a useful new feature is 'Library Lists'. There has always been the facility to create your own bookshelves but I wanted the ability to organise e-stock in thematic lists everyone could view. Browns acted on this and 'Library Lists' offer a way of grouping e-books by topic facilitating ease of discovery.

We have opted to allow everyone to view the full catalogue not just the stock we own. Students can select an option to email 'Suggestions for Purchase' to the Library. We download the MARC records for the e-books to our Access-IT library catalogue which enables users to click straight through to the VLeBooks interface.

Promoting e-books

It is crucial to have an ongoing campaign of promotion to raise awareness of the e-book stock. There is a tendency for them to be overlooked as they are not browsable and obvious in the way physical books are. Twitter (@welly_library) and emails to pupils highlighting new e-books are one way of reaching some library users. I created posters advertising subject specific e-book stock and put them up in the academic departments as well as shelf signs mentioning that an e-version of a particular book is also available in addition to the print copy.

Lessons Learnt

- We have adopted a very flexible approach to e-books – offering them as an option to stretch Sixth Formers in the subjects they are passionate about
- Where possible we buy licences via the credit system to enable multiple users to read the same book simultaneously (helpful in the classroom setting)
- We buy popular fiction and prize lists – Carnegie, Booker Prize, Bailey's Prize where the e-books are available
- We have had successes in responding to EPQ and Extended Essay topic requests with e-books (i.e. not specific titles)
- Rapid response to requests for books and information via e-books and the ability to read on smart phones is a big selling point.

Cambridge Companions Online – PDF versions of Companions to Philosophy, Religion, Literature, Classics and Music

We also have access to a large collection of e-books through our Cambridge Companions online (http://universitypublishingonline.org/cambridge/companions). This extensive collection of e-books is very well-used by our English, History and Philosophy departments. The librarians have demonstrated the main features of this collection to individuals and classes in the library. This e-resource has proved particularly useful for coursework and the Extended Essay and EPQs. The catalogue record can be imported into a library management system and references can be generated at the click of a button.

To sum up, we are not currently being inundated by requests for e-books. However, having the option to offer e-books and respond to book requests rapidly is valuable. We have demonstrated the e-book platform in tutorial sessions, to small groups, to academic department meetings and individuals. Usage reports can be accessed and it is clear that use is increasing. I see this as a long-term project and as the e-book stock expands we have more to offer. I do not intend to purchase e-textbooks in a comprehensive way until they demonstrate considerable added value over the printed versions.

Conclusion

Being able to offer a wide-range of e-resources to Sixth Formers for their extended projects, coursework and essays is mutually beneficial. Not only does it enhance the quality and range of sources they include in their written work but it raises the profile of the Library and demonstrates to students our relevance and usefulness.

It is an excellent way of assisting students in the transition from school to university. Not only do we familiarise them with digital resources they will encounter at university such as JSTOR and Cambridge Companions but they are learning to widen and narrow searches and filter by date, source type and so on.

Recommendations

My personal recommendations would be that if you have the budget to offer e-books then find the platform to suit your school. Consider what your priorities are for your own particular setting. Be prepared to start small and keep growing the e-book collection. Promotion needs to be ongoing and relentless – revel in the small successes. Be enthused when one teacher or pupil is genuinely impressed or excited at the book pinging onto the virtual bookshelf on their smart phone or tablet. Success will only come through word-of-mouth. School libraries need to be at the cutting edge of technology and librarians need to know what's out there and how to use it.

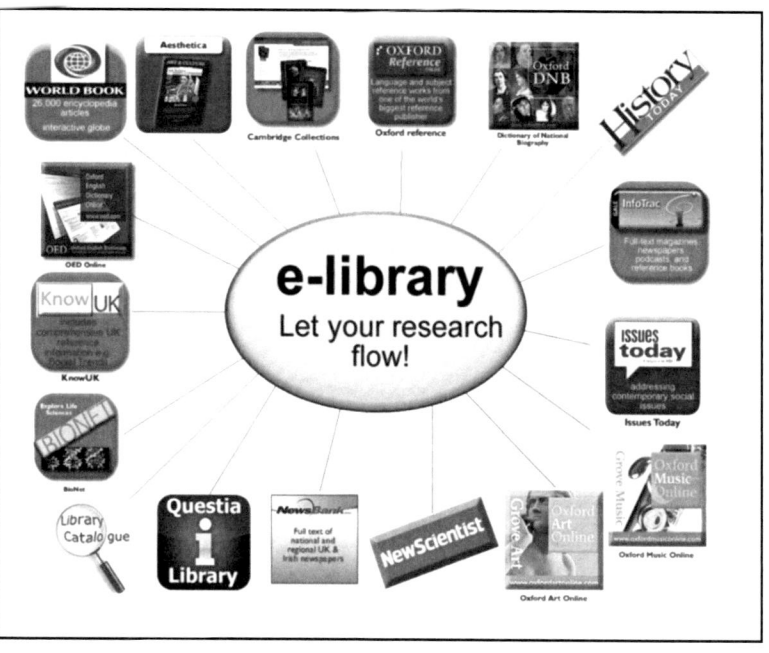

Poster promoting the e-Library

Concerning e-libraries: if your budget is limited try to choose one or two key general resources that will really enhance your students' access to scholarly, academic online sources. If possible work with your local library service and register your pupils to have access to the many useful e-resources they often offer.

We ran a workshop for Sixth Form parents to highlight our e-resources and demonstrate how we support their Y12 and 13s. They were impressed, vowing to go home and encourage their youngsters to use the library, one described the e-Library as 'an embarrassment of riches'.

There's no point having expensive and impressive e-resources if nobody knows about them!

Educational Online resource suppliers

- Cambridge Information http://www.caminfo.co.uk/index.html
- JCS https://www.jcsonlineresources.org/

Editor's note: the SLA has a Guideline on the subject of e-resources: *Digital Decisions: Selecting and Using e-resources in the Secondary School Library* (2016)

Case Study 4

Read. Research. Revise: Moving to Higher Education – A Seamless Transition

Rosalind Buckland

Librarian, Ripley St Thomas C E Academy, Lancaster; SLA Board member; Chair of SLA Lancashire Branch; SLYA Honour List 2012

Ripley St Thomas Church of England Academy is a large school in Lancaster with 1,750 pupils. Ripley was founded in 1864 by Julia and Thomas Ripley, a gift to the young people of Lancaster and Liverpool. The Academy is a Teaching School, a National Support School and a School-Centred Initial Teacher Training (SCITT) school and was judged outstanding by Ofsted in every category in 2011. Ripley has a strong church foundation and aims to develop its young people in body, mind and spirit. A particular focus is placed on personal development and service. Ripley provides a mainly academic curriculum and a wealth of extracurricular activities for its pupils. Significant premises' development in recent years has included a state of the art library, the John Crewdson Library (JCL), next to the Sixth Form building, which opened in July 2014. The original library, located a short distance away on another part of the campus, services the lower school.

As librarian I was invited to provide ideas for the internal layout of the JCL which has been designed to provide a range of learning environments that complement different learning styles. These include: ICT provision through fixed PCs or through other devices using Wi-Fi, a custom made workbench, tables, and a soft seat area with leather sofas. Students also have the opportunity to use a sound-proofed classroom that houses a 'CTouch' interactive television screen.

The Sixth Form library provision has been influenced by my experience as an Information Officer at a university library and is intended to provide a natural environment for students to read, research, and revise. The higher education (HE) library model is appropriate as 90% of our students go on to study at university, and in this context the JCL contributes towards a seamless transition into HE libraries and learning.

In addition to the JCL, students have access to a separate room dedicated to silent study. Therefore, the focus of the JCL is to offer opportunities for collaborative learning, which means students are welcome to communicate, *quietly*.

Contributing to a seamless transition into HE involves a self-check kiosk, part of the 3M RFID security system which enables students to issue and discharge their own books. This has proven to be effective in ensuring students are accountable for their borrowing.

As one might expect of modern library provision, the JCL offers a mix of book and non-book media, as well as magazines and daily newspapers. Investment in digital resources is a major objective, the result of a growing acknowledgement by us to ensure our students are equipped with the appropriate resources to undertake online research.

The promotion of the JCL and its resources is undertaken in various ways; during assemblies, on the Sixth Form plasma screen, and the Sixth Form bulletin. In addition, the JCL also has its own 'Twitter' account which I administer through 'Hootsuite', a social media management system.

Library Provision: Overview

Fiction book stock and reading for pleasure

The majority of the fiction book collection is student-led in that books are either requested or recommended by students. 'Request & Recommend' boxes are situated around the JCL and books are ordered to satisfy these requests. Upon the books' arrival, students are notified and given the option to be the first to borrow them. This practice ensures currency and suitability of fiction book stock, and consolidates the JCL's role in satisfying students' needs. A sticker displaying the student's name is added to the front of these books, which is an effective form of peer endorsement that also promotes reading for pleasure.

The e-book revolution

Having investigated various methods of e-reading, which included trialling two e-book platforms, it was apparent that the biggest hurdles to implementation included: funding; access to Wi-Fi; the provision of devices; and the barriers relating to the Digital Rights Management (DRM). Therefore, as the JCL has excellent Wi-Fi combined with the fact that the majority of Sixth Form students have their own devices, it may be that the Bring Your Own Device (BYOD) might be the most appropriate course of action. However, this is still work in progress and is included in the JCL's long term development plan. This decision is made easier by the fact that no single e-book platform provider can satisfy all students' book requests.

In contrast, and as one would expect, Lancashire County Library offers excellent e-reading facilities. Becoming a member is a simple process that can be undertaken online and does not require a signature or parental consent. Therefore, Sixth Form students who wish to access e-books are encouraged to consider using Lancashire Libraries as the volume of e-books available on its catalogue is vast, and as such, it is a resource that can complement our school collections.

Despite this ease of access and its wealth of resources, the biggest challenge remains persuading students to join. The JCL helps to promotes Lancashire Library membership by inviting representatives from Lancashire Libraries to visit, stocking their literature and embedding their weblinks on the LMS.

However, it should be noted, in a recent online survey (undertaken July 2015), although 32% of our students own a Kindle or e-reader, when asked to select their preferred reading materials, books (56%) were by far the preferred choice followed by magazines (20%), with only 4% choosing a Kindle or e-reader.

RAYS (Read Around Your Subject)

Non-fiction book stock is comprised of text books and titles that Subject Leaders (SL) (formerly known as Heads of Departments) recommend for wider reading around their subjects. This ensures that all the current non-fiction book stock is relevant and as a result, very much used. This relevance also encourages SLs to promote these books during lessons through the distribution of the JCL's, customised subject specific reading lists. These are available in full colour, hard copy leaflets which are inserted into books and also displayed in a dedicated rack.

In addition, as each book is tagged in the LMS, these reading lists can be produced as a search result or, extracted in the form of a QR code or weblink which can be embedded in an email or blog.

These read around your subject reading lists, with the RAYS acronym and logo, helps to promote this initiative and distinguish RAYS books from other JCL stock.

Subject Leaders bring their classes to the JCL to show students the location of their subject's RAYS.

Students are also encouraged to visit and use the JCL through its recent adoption of Subjects' class sets of text books. Previously, it was common practice for these books which are loaned to students for the duration of the academic year, to be kept in the Subjects' departments. These books are now kept in the JCL and catalogued on the LMS with a default two week loan period which means students either renew online by remote access to their LMS account, or alternatively they visit the JCL and renew using the 3M self-check kiosk.

Non-fiction periodicals and journals are also stocked, many of which are available in digital format. The JCL currently carries twelve journal titles. Upon receipt of each new volume a colour photocopy of the front cover and the contents page is distributed to the respective SL's departments for display in the classrooms.

Information Literacy

Context

Beyond what they do with individual teachers in subject lessons, the extent of most students' prior knowledge of Information Literacy (IL) is limited to their ICT lessons in KS3, and to those pupils who undertook ICT at GCSE. As a result, the majority of Sixth Form students have little knowledge or experience of IL. Owing to an increased awareness amongst teaching colleagues of the need to demonstrate to examination boards the extent to which their students have undertaken research and acknowledged information sources, I am invited to deliver IL lessons. Subjects I am invited to work with are those that are traditionally associated with written coursework such as the humanities.

Appropriate Tools

With so little material on the world wide web intended for educational purposes, the JCL's investment in digital research databases is proving invaluable, as provenance, currency, and to a certain extent suitability, can be assumed as given for these resources and therefore, reduces the time required to undertake research. This investment also contributes to our overarching aim of a seamless transition to HE as all university libraries host research databases and using these databases enables our students to develop some of sophisticated independent learning skills that they will need for university level work.

The IL lessons which are part of the students' directed time are delivered in two parts. The first lesson is an introduction to academic research databases and their ability to link with PDFs, HTML, video, graphics, and sound. This session includes instruction on how to undertake effective searches using filters such as advanced search, Boolean, and the importance of creating and then working to agreed time schedules. Students learn how to create digital folders and how to tag, store, save and extract results for future reference. The second lesson focusses on how to cite and reference, using either the Harvard or Numeric conventions, dependent upon the wishes of the subject teacher. Not only do students gain an understanding of how to avoid plagiarism, but also appreciate that by acknowledging information sources they are demonstrating the extent to which they have researched their subject.

Another advantage of these databases is that they offer the administrator the ability to extract usage reports that measure the number of times the database has been accessed and also a search history of the topics and keywords researched. These reports can be auto generated weekly or monthly and are useful to consolidate usage and justify investment.

Badged Open Courses (BOCs)

A recent string to our IL bow has been the discovery of the Open University's Digital Literacy BOC, a resource that is open source (freely available) on the OpenLearn platform. The access level of the BOCs are GCSEs and beyond and in addition to Digital Literacy the range of BOCs provided by the OU include: Maths, English for Study, Succeed in the Workplace, and First Steps into HE.

The Digital Literacy BOC is designed to help students develop the skills for effective online learning: searching efficiently and critically evaluating information etc. BOCs offer students the flexibility to undertake the course at their convenience and so following the initial session, unless otherwise required, students continue to work independently. BOCs have great potential as not only do they offer students the opportunity to gain new skills, they also provide evidence of their achievement in the form of an Open University 'digital badge' that can be included in CVs and personal statements.

Information Literacy: Extended Project Qualification (EPQ)

For students undertaking their Extended Project Qualification (EPQ), the IL sessions form the foundation of a more sophisticated research programme which involves additional taught sessions and visits to a university library – the result of a collaborative partnership with our local HE provider which is now in its seventh year. As an EPQ supervisor, I am able to appreciate the extent to which IL is a major component in developing students' ability to undertake effective research.

Collaborative Partnership

Our partnership with the University of Cumbria involves a series of reciprocal visits where Learning Advisors visit our Sixth Form and our students visit the university library. The latter involves a taught session in an ICT lab which includes an introduction to the University's vast repository of databases. The visit also includes a guided tour of the library and its physical resources. This offers students an opportunity to gain an insight into HE library provision and discover the extent to which the digital dimension of learning is practiced and as such, these visits provide an excellent form of enrichment.

The Learning Advisers (or equivalent) who are usually associated with libraries within the university are keen to work with schools and Sixth Form colleges, in order to highlight the benefits of HE as a key strand of universities' Outreach remit. Most universities have similar Outreach departments and welcome contact from schools.

Other examples of our collaborative partnerships include our work with the English and Linguistics Society at Lancaster University. Our students are welcome to attend the Society's prestigious events with guest speakers such as Professor David Crystal.

Information Literacy: Evaluation

Undertaking an evaluation of the library provision for our Sixth Formers, resources (physical and digital), as well as IL lessons, is invaluable, and has included the gate counter footfall, desk based statistics, anecdotal feedback, and Survey Monkey questionnaires. The Academy subscribes to Survey Monkey which enables results to be extracted in accessible formats (PowerPoint, Excel, Word, and pdf). Students are invited to indicate those resources that offer the greatest potential. Their assessments are essential to our decision making and future planning, especially with regards to the renewal or cancellation of subscriptions.

Findings from these evaluations confirm the success, or otherwise, of our investment in digital resources. Students are comfortable with the digital dimension of learning and evidence of their use of digital resources is reflected in the quality of their work.

In addition to the data I gather, each of the databases offers the facility to extract usage statistics for desk based research. This information helps determine which resources are of greatest value. Findings from evaluations can be used to validate past or future investment.

Digital Research Databases: Funding

Reallocation of funds

In an ideal world, I believe that the majority of Sixth Form librarians would subscribe to a suite of digital resources as our HE counterparts do. However, these resources are costly items in relation to an often modest annual budget. Therefore, the most obvious path may be to reallocate funding, reduce investment in the physical, non-fiction book stock in favour of those that are digital. My loan statistics vindicate such a decision as there has been a steady decline in non-fiction borrowing over recent years.

Consolidation of budgets

The majority of our Subject Leaders do not need to be persuaded of the merits of subject specific, digital databases and so, where circumstances allow, it has been a deliberate policy to bring together elements of different school budgets. Along with a proportion of the library's budget we have included contributions from the school's Literacy, Extended Project Qualification, and Enrichment budgets in order to provide funding for these important digital resources.

Consortia

Many leading digital resource suppliers offer discounts for multi buys, and some for a cluster, or consortium of colleges or schools. These are always worth investigating. The supplier will generally indicate which schools in your county, not just in your immediate area, are wanting to co-invest. We have been fortunate in this respect as a neighbouring school expressed a like-minded interest in a particular resource which resulted in a favourable discount. Without this consortium, this product would not have been affordable.

Meeting our Stakeholders' Needs

Collectively, our cross-curricular digital resources budget is helping us to maintain our current level of investment in the digital dimension of learning. These research databases combined with BOCs, membership to the County Library, the embedding of weblinks into the LMS's homepage – most universities host excellent digital IL resources the majority of which are now open source – and our collaborative partnership with our local HE providers, complements our efforts to enhance and broaden our students' e-learning.

For anyone unsure of where to begin, or which resources to invest in, the SLA's annual conference provides excellent opportunities to visit trade stands and speak directly with suppliers. In addition, sector specific information can be found in many of the SLA's publications.

The digital dimension to learning is second nature for today's Sixth Form students, or 'digital natives' as they are also known, therefore, it is common sense to ensure attempts are made to service their needs. At Ripley St Thomas we acknowledge this to be a priority. Through identifying the potential this dimension of learning can offer, and implementing the appropriate resources, we are enriching the read, research, and revise aspect of our students' library and learning.

Case Study 5

Designing a Library Space for Sixth Form

Lesley Martin

Librarian, Culford School, Bury St Edmunds

My school is an independent day and boarding school in Suffolk with a roll of around 380 in the Senior School (Y9–13) in addition to the Prep and Pre-Prep schools that share the site.

The previous school library was in a beautiful wood panelled Edwardian room at the back of the Hall (think National Trust stately home). When this first became the school library in 1972 it was an ideal place for it. Most teaching still took place in the main building, the Hall. In the library there was space for bookcases and study tables to seat about 35 pupils, and in the 1990s a computer suite was added which proved very popular both with individuals and for classes. The school appointed its first professional librarian in 1996 and when I joined in 2001 there was already talk of relocating the library. It was becoming more and more clear that the library could not keep pace with the developments in teaching and learning at the school. Gradually teaching departments moved out of the Hall to newer classroom blocks on the far side of the building from the library. Departments obtained their own computer suites and so no longer brought classes to the library. English classes still came for reading time and to exchange books but Sixth Formers, with few exceptions, preferred to go elsewhere for private study. It also proved almost impossible to access reliable WiFi, increasingly important as we moved away from providing suites of computers towards expecting pupils to use their own laptops. Despite my best efforts, library use was gradually dwindling and although I was able to halt the decline to a certain extent, we could see that in another decade or so the library would moulder away altogether.

Action was required. In 2011 the Governors approved the plan to build a new library and the exciting process of inviting architects to tender began. I was fortunate to have input into the brief, the process of choosing the architects, and my opinions were sought in subsequent meetings. It is also useful that the Headmaster and I had reasonably similar aspirations for the new building. It was to be as future proof as we could make it, a flexible space where multiple activities could occur simultaneously, a space to encourage reading and promote independent learning. This was a focus of the school development plan. The Headmaster was keen for the new library to be the 'academic heart of the school' and in his 2015 Speech Day address said, I quote, *'The new library offers us the opportunity to enhance [independent learning] yet further for our Sixth Form pupils especially, giving them a university-style academic facility combined with all the support that a pastorally focused school can offer. The mezzanine floor will be an area reserved exclusively for the Sixth Form and we are installing a coffee facility as part of our effort to offer them an adult working environment. It should be a first class environment for quiet thought or reading; for general conversations about academic work or the world at large; or for individual study and the production of work to reflect the outcomes of that reflection, reading and dialogue.'*

The architects produced an exciting plan with a double height glass walled foyer leading to a large open plan space with a lecture theatre and mezzanine level above. As soon as I saw the mezzanine on the plans I had mentally earmarked it for Sixth Form use, and so, it turned out, had the Headmaster. Two of our priorities throughout the project were planning for independent learning and Sixth Form – both in terms of encouraging them to make better use of their independent learning time (Private Study or PS) and in preparing them for the university library and learning environment. Our Senior School serves Y9 – 13, and Sixth Form recruitment and retention is important. In planning a new library therefore we were keen to make it more of a university style experience than a school one. We researched school and university libraries, looking at the learning commons model particularly, and the Headmaster visited several school and university libraries during a trip to Australia. We also ran focus groups with the pupils, getting feedback from School Council and the Pupil Academic Committee about what they wanted. Sixth Formers were keen to have an area specifically for them as one of the complaints about the current library was that younger pupils coming in and out disturbed them, and if there was an English class in the library there was often nowhere for Sixth Form to work, and it felt crowded. The Headmaster and I were both keen on the idea of a coffee bar although we could not work out the logistics of it and were concerned about noise, smell and mess. In the end we have installed a coffee machine and hot water dispenser so pupils can make their own drinks. This is working well and the Sixth Form Committee

Super Sixes

have taken responsibility for making sure the kitchen area is left clean and tidy (mostly!). A former pupil who left last year came in to have a look at the finished product, having watched it being built all last year, and commented that it had the same sort of feel as her university library. She also said, 'I wish this had been here for me – I might have done some more work!'

Location was a key issue and the site chosen is ideal; adjacent to the main teaching blocks and *en route* to the boarding houses and dining hall. The entire senior school passes the new library at least six times a day and the glass front of the building is a showcase for all going on within.

The library is zoned following the design of the building. The glass foyer is the social learning area with comfy seating and browser displays of featured books. We also used it for our first lunchtime event, a poetry open mic to celebrate National Poetry Day. The circulation desk marks the transition to the main area of the library where we have two large 'doughnut' shaped low bookshelves for the fiction and some comfy seats for reading. The non-fiction is around the walls. We kept the building neutral with white walls, grey flooring and wooden bookshelves on the walls, to go with the wooden glulam beams which are a feature of the design, and have used bright and zingy colours and interesting curvy shapes for the soft furnishings and freestanding bookshelves.

Towards the back of the room we have two large standing tables for group work – there are also high stools here and many pupils like to use these tables to study at. In the old library, the books were in bays around the room and while there were

study tables in the main room, many pupils preferred to use the annexe room, where the computers were located. Issues have increased by a third since the new library opened and one reason for this I believe is that pupils can look up from their study and see the books immediately. The increased shelf space means that I can have many more books on face out display making them more obvious and many more pupils are using them, including Sixth Form. In fact a quick check of Sixth Form issues in the six weeks since we opened show that not only are they borrowing more books, but a large proportion of them are non-fiction to support their studies. From where they sit on the mezzanine level they have a fantastic view of all the non-fiction books. We have also had self-service units put in and pupils like the autonomy of being able to issue their own books, although I rather miss seeing what they are taking out and using the opportunity to chat to them about their reading.

The Lecture Theatre can seat 80 but has a dividing wall to turn it into two separate rooms. It did not take long for the Sixth Form to ask if they could use these rooms for silent study, group work, or to practise presentations. We have now added some tables to these rooms so they can be used as study rooms when required.

The mezzanine has three large sofas, coffee tables and stools, and six study tables which seat five or six pupils at each. A Sixth Form Collection of books – both fiction and non-fiction – is being built up gradually. I decided against putting A Level texts upstairs, partly because they are rather large, but mainly because I felt I wanted to develop a collection to extend their reading beyond the curriculum. So the collection comprises narrative non-fiction on a range of subjects, based on our Sixth Form and Scholars' reading lists and the reading lists supplied by various universities, and adult fiction such as the Costa and Man Booker shortlists and previous winners. I am also encouraging Sixth Formers to recommend books to one another and to start a reading group.

We have a relatively large Sixth Form who are required to remain on site during the school day even during private study periods. (We are in a rural location so there is really nowhere for them to go.) Previously boarders could go to their bedrooms, and a study room was provided for day pupils in each house. In addition the Sixth Form Centre was also available to them at certain times. Only pupils whose tutors felt they were not keeping up with academic work were required to work in the library. It was, however, noted that pupils might be more interested in socialising than studying during these times as supervision is light in the boarding houses during the day. Now, however, all Lower Sixth pupils are required to be in the library during their PS. One of our Housemasters recently commented, 'It is great to see them actually working in the library. Previously many of them would have been in their rooms playing games and wasting time.' Upper Sixth may choose where to study and many of them are choosing to come to the library – even in preference to the new coffee shop which has opened in our sports centre! I can't think of a bigger endorsement than that.

Quotes from Sixth Formers

'I love the purple sofas. I enjoy being able to kick my shoes off, put my feet up, and drink a coffee while I study.'

'It is nice and bright and airy. It's good to have our own space where we're not disturbed by the younger pupils.'

'The furniture is really cool and I love the different shapes and colours.'

'Coming to the library means I actually get on with my prep (homework) where if I went to the House I'd just be chatting to my friends.'

'I didn't realise the library had so many books which would be useful for my studies.'

Case Study 6

Man Booker Prize Shadowing: Re-discovering Reading for Pleasure by establishing a Sixth Form Book Club

James Curtis
Librarian, Holland Park School

Marissa Gisbourne
Previously Senior Librarian, Holland Park School

Holland Park is a co-educational comprehensive school, situated in the Royal Borough of Kensington and Chelsea, London. Recognised as an outstanding school by Ofsted the school exacts high standards from all students, and particularly those in the Sixth Form, where students are expected to achieve a grade A* or A at GCSE in the subjects they wish to study. There are over 1,300 students, including approximately 160 in the Sixth Form.

In September 2012 Holland Park was nearing the completion of a whole school rebuild that would include the provision of two new libraries; a Main Library to cater for the whole school community, with fiction and non-fiction that would appeal to and be suitable for all students and staff, and a Sixth Form Library, with adjacent study centre, that would serve the academic needs of Sixth Form students. We were both newly employed at Holland Park from September in order to launch these libraries and develop the service that the school wished to offer pupils. With the current educational agenda decidedly focused on students' achievement, together with enjoyment of literacy and literature, one of our main goals was to encourage and nurture whole-school love of reading for pleasure. One of our priorities was to be the Sixth Form.

Context

In the three months before moving into the new school building we began not only to dismantle what remained of the old library, but also introduced ourselves to the students around the school by conducting surveys with students and offering rewards for particularly constructive feedback. Talking with Sixth Formers and those on the school's Student Leadership Team we found that many students were keen to read and read widely, but did not know where to begin. This research continued once we had established ourselves in the new school building. As we tracked Sixth Form use of the library we began to realise that Sixth Form students did not use the library for anything that did not directly affect their studies. They rarely ventured outside of the Sixth Form Library (the bulk of the fiction collection is held in the school's Main Library so as to be accessible to all). Speaking informally with some students, time and again it appeared that although they felt they would like to read more for pleasure, they didn't really have time on top of their studies and, as such, had not made it one of their priorities. This was despite the fact that they could see how reading more widely would only be a positive influence on their education. With this in mind we thought that the Sixth Form, with their imminent departure for university and the wider world, were an important group to target as part of a much wider whole-school vision of reading initiatives and book clubs, which we were in the process of establishing.

Setting Up the Club

Parallel to setting up the Sixth Form Book Club we were, like many other school librarians across the country, setting up a Carnegie Shadowing Group, the first in the school's history. We were very clear in our minds that we did not want the Sixth Form Book Club to follow this sort of pattern. It was not to be a librarian-led affair with reading, activities and discussion guided by us. From our conversations with students and members of staff it was clear to us that the Sixth Formers would benefit most, and would probably be most attracted to, a club following a more traditional book club format, with casual discussion and a say in the choice of reading.

Our first challenge was advertising the club. As we were effectively starting from scratch we naturally employed some of the more common ways of advertising throughout school: plasma screens, notices to tutor groups, and the Sixth Form newsletter. We supplemented this with targeted visits to English classes and tutor groups, allowing us the opportunity to personally deliver the message to students and engage with them further about what the group might be, and through personal invitations to those students who had expressed a desire to join or whom teachers had told us might be interested in the group. The personal invitation strategy proved particularly effective; students felt a greater personal connection to the club and an immediate sense of involvement. It also meant they brought along friends who might not have otherwise considered attending.

Precisely how we would manage the club, and how we would finance it, were closely intertwined. The school is lucky to benefit from the Holland Park Trust, a charitable body that provides grants for specific projects that might not otherwise be possible within the school budget. We were able to secure funding from the Trust for the Sixth Form Book Club and other reading initiatives. One of the key points of our application, and indeed the driving force behind the club, was to reignite our students' love of reading. We decided to purchase copies of books for the students, rather than sourcing them from reading group sets available from our local library service, as we had done with other younger book groups. This choice was open to us because of the funding we had been successful in bidding for, and had two major positive advantages for what we wanted to achieve with the book club. Firstly we were not limited in what books we, or the students, might want to read in the group. Secondly, buying the books for students to keep, as well as removing the problems of keeping track of group borrowing sets (always something of a logistical nightmare within school reading groups), gave students something to retain, a memento of their time in the book club to take away with them to the next stage of their education. A sense of ownership of the books allowed students to feel some ownership of the club itself, and gave the group a sense that this was not simply a library-directed initiative, but a group whose primary function was the discussion of great books.

We wanted to make the main focus of the group a reminder of the joy of reading for pleasure. Talking with students prior to setting up the club we had been confronted with a group who wanted to read, but whose desire and engagement in reading had been somewhat dampened by their GCSE studies and by the increased workload of the Sixth Form. We wanted to use the group to introduce students to challenging, stimulating, and quality contemporary literature and, by giving them a say in what we read, a greater autonomy over their reading. Up to this point most students we spoke to had been so engrossed in their studies that only those who were already keen readers were reading beyond the set texts covered in GCSE and A level English. By offering students something off-curriculum, as it were, we were offering them the chance to engage in something new to them. It was this idea that led us to becoming involved in shadowing the 2013 Man Booker Prize.

Going beyond the books: the Man Booker Prize and Author Visits

Having decided that the group would endeavour to explore predominantly contemporary literature it seemed a natural move that we might begin by shadowing the Man Booker Prize. Allowing students to pick and choose from the long and shortlists gave them a soft introduction to some of the best of contemporary literature and enabled us to have multiple, diverse, discussions. Students committed to reading at least one of the shortlist over the Summer holidays. Each selected a different title that appealed so that at least one group

Super Sixes

member would have read each title being considered for the Award. This gave us enough time to meet, discuss our favourites and recommend other titles to one another before the big event that we had organised for early in the academic year. In an effort to extend the impact of the club beyond the books, and indeed beyond the club itself, we contacted the Man Booker Prize press office, and were able to secure a visit from one of the judges of that year's panel, Natalie Haynes, an author, journalist and broadcaster who was in the process of publishing her debut novel.

Our engagement directly with the prize allowed our students to feel a great sense of connection with the books they were reading. The event, an intimate gathering of the club, a select group of students from the lower school, and staff was a great success. Natalie Haynes was fantastic and students and staff alike were rapt by her insights into the world of literary prizes and publishing. She discussed briefly herself and her career, and then talked about judging the prize, the process and the level of commitment required to judge. Students were encouraged to ask questions throughout and so the event became much like an informal book club discussion, albeit on a larger scale, making the prize and its books seem more accessible and appealing to students. The presence of other students and members of staff at the event became an excellent opportunity, not just for the library to show its contribution to school life, but also to strengthen cross-curricular ties. Unlike with a traditional author visit, the dialogue of the works shortlisted for the prize allowed most literary styles and tastes to come up for discussion. Refreshments at the end of the events allowed students to mingle with our guest and ask questions on a more personal level, which opened up long talks about reading in general.

The success of this first event, and the connection formed with Natalie Haynes led to a second visit, where she kindly returned to discuss her background in Classics and her recently released novel, which tells the story of a modern day Greek tragedy. This visit afforded us the opportunity to again promote reading for pleasure amongst Sixth Form and in particular strengthen ties with the Latin classes. The event was also particularly successful in attracting a group of students who had previously shadowed the Carnegie with us, but who now, being KS4 students, were beginning to look for reading material and experiences more appropriate to their age, and to prepare them for Sixth Form entry. It was at this point that we began to realise the need for consistent recruitment to the club, if it were to continue. Our initial group of students would, mostly, be leaving at the end of the academic year, leaving us few in number if we did not begin to recruit and interest those soon to enter the Sixth Form. Such events became invaluable in our connection with the wider school and securing a continuation of the group for the coming years.

Problems and Pitfalls

Inevitably we experienced some problems that we needed to address, some more challenging than others.

- Starting with a bang: the Man Booker Prize cannot visit you every year. While the visit was key to our initial early success and visibility as a school club it also meant we had created a rod for our own backs, with the need to continue offering such events critical in the continued success of the club.

- Attendance was hard to guarantee at all meetings. While understandable – students do lead busy lives – this presented some difficulty in having enjoyable discussions about the books (this point also applies on the occasions that students may not have read the complete novel). We worked around this by enacting a 'first come' policy, whereby a set number of books was purchased for the club and those students who attended the last meeting (or those who had sent their apologies) were first to receive a copy, with other members of the group receiving a copy on a first come-first served basis. This immediately led to students treating the group with greater courtesy and maturity, and helped them appreciate it as something of a luxury.

- Giving the group free rein to choose the books discussed as a collective led to much discussion and disagreement, sometimes as much time as we spent discussing the book itself. We found that a guiding hand and a level of direction was still needed.

- Setting the tone: an unexpected challenge was the need to set the appropriate tone for meetings. Students took to the relative informality of the group structure with ease, but the discussions themselves were initially hampered by them treating it like a classroom discussion. While we had to do our homework and develop discussion points in case things flagged, we wanted students to respond personally to the books, not as if they were analysing a text in their English class. This was something that gradually disappeared as students became more accustomed to the change in style of the discussion.

- Student retention and moving forward: one problem already highlighted was the need to keep students interested in the club for the next year, but also to replace those members who would be leaving the school at the end of the year. Initially we followed our tactics in setting up the club – visiting English classes and sending out targeted invites. In recent years however we have begun to expand our reading group provision in school. We found that a Carnegie shadowing group and a Sixth Form Book Club were such disparate things that a middle ground was needed. This has led to the formation of a 'Senior' Book Club, made up primarily of Year 11 and Year 10 students. This club has very similar aims to the Sixth Form Group, and allows students to read quality and challenging literature in a supportive environment outside of the classroom. This group has developed into a recruiting ground for the Sixth Form Book Club, with members advancing into the more senior club as they move up through the school.

Successes and Feedback

The Sixth Form book club became well established and understood through these events. During the first year of its existence the group read 10 literary titles which the students were allowed to keep – in the case where they had not enjoyed it they happily donated their copy back to the library. This was a really important part of the scheme as, though the tone was set, moving forward the group chose titles they wanted to read and discuss from a list of suggestions we complied for each meeting. We thought this provided a good balance as, while students had considerable input over what we would be reading, leaving the selecting of a shortlist of titles to us kept us focussed on the club's original goal. Moving on from the Man Booker prize, we looked at some other literary awards, as well as a list of modern classics, books you 'should know about' amongst others. This became a particularly successful way of increasing the students' knowledge of literature not on the curriculum, and opening up lively debate about genres, tastes and successful plots. The fact that they were keeping the books meant they had a greater desire to select a book they know they would read.

Feedback at the end of the year from students was that their book knowledge had increased, that they had enjoyed the social and intellectual challenge and that the events organised along with the group had inspired them to read more, and to read better quality literature.

The following comments were taken from student feedback, presented to the Holland Park Trust, in thanks for the funding of the book club:

'The book club has been a most wonderful addition to our academic and social lives. It is one of the most thriving Sixth Form societies and we thoroughly enjoy the meetings…'

'The book club has provided me and the other members with an opportunity to explore literature both modern and classic that we would never have before considered.'

Super Sixes

'Book Club has been a wonderful experience this past year. It has allowed me to not only read books I perhaps would not have chosen otherwise, but to discuss (and sometimes even argue about) the books, giving me an opportunity to see the stories from a totally different perspective.'

Books Read

These are the initial ten titles that students were able to keep, including the six books from the Man Booker Prize 2013 shortlist and Natalie Hayne's debut novel.

- *London Fields* – Martin Amis
- *We Need New Names* – NoViolet Bulawayo
- *The Luminaries* – Eleanor Catton
- *Harvest* – Jim Crace
- *The Amber Fury* – Natalie Haynes
- *One Flew Over the Cuckoo's Nest* – Ken Kesey
- *The Lowland* – Jhumper Lahiri
- *A Tale for the Time Being* – Ruth Ozeki
- *NW* – Zadie Smith
- *The Testament of Mary* – Colm Tóibín

Case Study 7

Working with Birmingham University in a Subject Context: Research Support for A Level History

Helen Emery BA (Hons) MSc

Librarian and Resource Centre Manager/Co-ordinator for Literacy Across the Curriculum, King Edward VI School, Lichfield
also Chair – SLA Staffordshire Branch

Introduction

When I was asked to write this case study I questioned what I could possibly have to share about my work with our Sixth Form which would be of any use to fellow professionals. However, through speaking to our Sixth Formers and subsequently reflecting on my work, I have realised that sharing our practice has much more of an impact on our school library colleagues than we often realise. Our school is by no means a perfect scenario but my hope is that through reading what we do at King Edward VI School, Lichfield it will encourage you with your work amongst your own Sixth Form students.

Context

Students studying A level History at King Edward's follow the AQA specification which includes the Historical Enquiry unit studied by both of our two Year 13 groups.

Following successful liaison with teaching staff in the History Department on some Key Stage 3 research activities, the Head of Department approached me to ask what support we could offer to enhance the experience for our students with this type of very independent essay.

I am aware that this level of proactivity from a Head of Department is rare, and I feel exceedingly blessed that this particular department has an understanding of the Library facility and what it can offer. I am also fortunate that the teaching staff are very keen for their students to benefit from the service too. If you are working in a school with staff who are less willing to work together with you, I would suggest simply finding one teacher with one class to work with. Then hopefully the ripple effect will happen to the rest of the department – and possibly other departments – as they share how fantastic the Library is! (I must add there are departments in this school who I do not work as closely with.)

Liaison with the staff was kept very informal – in my experience formal meetings create a sense of extra workload and I was keen that the busy teaching staff did not see my involvement as an additional burden. We simply emailed or caught up in free lessons – it was highly advantageous that the History department classrooms are all located next to the LRC!

What also helped this particular project was that the requirements of the Historical Enquiry include elements which are directly applicable to information literacy skills, which we in the LRC aim to develop in students. Assessment criteria include that 'a range of sources is considered and evaluated'[18] and that students must 'analyse and evaluate a range of appropriate source material with discrimination'[19] – ideal for the LRC to have a real impact.

I feel it is appropriate here to expand a little further on the specific information literacy skills which this essay required. Students were – under the guidance of their teacher – to choose an historical issue to investigate within the context of a 100-year time frame. This could focus on the role and significance of key personalities, candidates could investigate the causes, consequences and significance of important events or the piece could be thematically based.[20] Most of our students focused on some aspect of the reign of French Monarchs in the context of the French Revolution. Whatever their chosen question, marks are given to students for demonstrating three areas related to information literacy which we were able to impact upon.

- Students needed to use a *range of sources* – in my experience students are only too ready to use the first couple of pieces of information they come across and leave it at that. The LRC is the ideal place to introduce students to a wider selection of sources than their set text book or Wikipedia (neither of these may I add are objectionable in themselves – they just should not be used at the exclusivity of other sources).

- *Relevant selection of material/precisely selected evidence* – this links to the previous criteria, encouraging students to assess which information to use and which to leave out.

- *Analysis and evaluation of sources* – students need to specifically include a source evaluation section in their essay which requires them to compare each interpretation of past events and how they differ. Again, the LRC focuses on considering the merits and pitfalls of different information sources and students were supported in that.

The final area is more general, but *quality of written communication* also carries marks. Attention to spelling, punctuation and grammar are essential and as the Literacy Across the Curriculum coordinator in school I can support students in reaching high standards in this area.

Laying the Foundations

Our first step was to hold a very simple 30-minute introductory session for both groups taking the course, led by me in the Library Resource Centre. This enabled me to make explicit the link between independent research and the service offered by the LRC. There is often a perception amongst students that a school library is the sole domain of Key Stage 3 fiction, with Sixth Formers simply using it as a common room or worse, seeing no use in it at all and often not making use of my expertise.

With the Historical Enquiry forming 20% of the final A Level mark, students were able to see from the mark scheme how good research, supported by the Library and the service we offer, can significantly impact their grades. Although the final deadline is not until the February of Year 13, we held this initial session in the Summer term of Year 12, which gives students the opportunity to do some background reading over the Summer holidays. The session was within History curriculum time so student attendance wasn't voluntary – and the history teacher was present throughout. Support from the teaching staff meant we could in effect 'team teach' and give the students a real overview of what was to be expected of them for this essay.

In preparation for the session we (the Head of Department and I) had created a bibliography of Library stock which directly linked to the topic in question. This aided students during their initial selection of resources.

I was able to remind them how to use the Library Catalogue and provide a quick reminder of classification systems to find print stock. Also, making the point that all university libraries will have similar and that adept use of them is key.

To quote one student I asked, *'The LRC had an excellent range of Historians* [sic] *that helped me secure a good historical debate.'*[21] Had I not liaised with the Head of Department on the exact stock to carry, students may have left the session feeling that it was not directly relevant.

During this initial session I also talked through the advantages and disadvantages of online sources, suggesting websites which the teaching staff had recommended on the bibliography and also highlighted the use of Google Books. Once we had secured the students' confidence that the service will be of use during this piece of work, I was also able to build relationships with the students which encourages trust in us as knowledgeable Library staff. This meant they would feel able to come back and ask us for more help once they had started their research. Students did indeed often come back to us on an individual basis from their subsequent history lessons to find more resources.

'The library helped me to pick out and photocopy specific pages of History Review magazine – loved it!' [22]

Referencing Session

I felt that a subsequent session on referencing and plagiarism needed to be taught relatively early on in their project following the introductory session – I have had many experiences of students using resources for their initial research, only to come back later on needing to reference the work and not being able to find the book/quote/page number.

We provided the students with a referencing guide, which specially gave examples from a history context and I encouraged the students to practice writing references using the stock they had been reading from the initial session. The session even went down to the specifics of showing them how to make use of the footnotes facility in Word – which most of them had not used before.

This session also showed students the importance of the issues concerning plagiarism. I also pointed out the declaration they sign to confirm all work is their own. I was genuinely surprised at the lack of awareness of this issue from our Year 13 students – so my advice to you, as reader, is never presume they know it all already!

When asked how the LRC had helped their History studies one student reflected that the session *'taught us how to correctly reference our work, which is something we hadn't had to do before'*.

University of Birmingham

One of the major successful features in this project was the support offered by the University of Birmingham. Ideally located on the same train line as our school, we took advantage of one of the free Information Literacy sessions which are held on campus.[23] This not only gave students an opportunity to consider their research skills alongside students from other schools, it gave them an insight into the expectations around independent study in a University context.

If you are unable to physically access your local University Library and their facilities, University of Birmingham have made their resources available as a downloadable pack[24] and is an invaluable resource for any Sixth Form Information literacy teaching – they are not specific to any subject in particular, so can be used not only in a history context but for all Sixth Form study. The sessions can easily be delivered by School Librarians with very little preparation needed (We are all busy aren't we?!).

N.B. There is also a pack on referencing/academic writing which might be useful - we did not use this during our visit as I had already covered this in the previous session, however it is again an invaluable resource for any Sixth Form Library.[25]

Should you need more information on what Birmingham University Library offers to Sixth Form students I am sure they would be happy for you to contact them for help.

Wider Resources

Once students had done their initial reading and started to write their enquiry, we were aware that some of them needed additional resources more specific to their individual piece. The visit to University of Birmingham meant that following their taught session we could show students around the library, see the online catalogue and then take them directly to the books in question. We also made them aware of Electronic Journals which the University had available which I could not offer them in school. Many students then visited the Library on their own some weeks later, using the permission letter provided.[26] I believe the trip we organised as a group meant the students were more familiar with the University Library and were much more likely to return under their own steam to do additional study/make use of their wider resources. Again, with so many students from our school planning to go onto university, this has given them a very practical and confidence boosting foretaste of what is to come.

There was one occasion where a student wanted a specific text not available in the school library or at University of Birmingham – so I made use of the local public library inter library loan service. The student was completely unaware that this service even existed so it was definitely worth the small fee they charged!

Writing the Enquiry

As I mentioned, I asked students for their thoughts on how the LRC had helped them to gain the grade they hoped for on the Historical Enquiry. I was surprised to hear that many appreciated the quiet study environment of the LRC to actually get the study written. I had underestimated the role the Library can play in simply providing a supportive, studious environment for our Sixth Formers to work – so I would encourage you not to forget how important this can be for many students.

To quote one student, the LRC… *'provided a space with a perfect atmosphere in which to conduct my studies.'* [27]

As the deadline loomed, we found that students were using the LRC more and more to finish their assessment on time – and as we had built up that supportive relationship with students we were able to calm their stress and answer last minute proof-reading/formatting/referencing queries.

Conclusion

In order for our Libraries to become an integral part of the Sixth Form experience, we need to make the work we do directly relevant to their studies, and create opportunities where we can make explicit the benefits of what we offer to our students. The Historical Enquiry from the AQA syllabus was an ideal way of doing just that – whilst also supporting teaching staff who can sometimes be used to spoon feeding exam classes to simply achieve exam success. We, as information professionals, can show them how to support their students in gaining the best results. In essence we need to walk that fine line with our young people through the process of independent research – guiding them and holding their hands when needed, whilst still allowing them to explore alone and develop into life-long learners.

References

[18] AQA *Unit 4: Historical Enquiry* [online]. 2015. [Accessed 9 April 2015]. Available from: http://www.aqa.org.uk/subjects/history/as-and-a-level/history-2040/subject-content/unit-4-historical-enquiry

[19] Ibid.

[20] Ibid.

[21] Sixth Form student. Conversation. March 2015

[22] Sixth Form student. Conversation. March 2015

[23] University of Birmingham *Information and research skills* [online]. 2015. [Accessed 9 April 2015]. Available from: http://www.birmingham.ac.uk/libraries/fesupport/infoskills.aspx

[24] University of Birmingham *Research and Study Skills: Research and Evaluation: Student Pack* 2nd Edition [online]. 2015. [Accessed 9 April 2015]. Available from: http://www.birmingham.ac.uk/Documents/libraries/9674-library-skills-student-ext-1-aw-web.pdf

[25] University of Birmingham *Research and Study Skills: Academic Writing Student Pack* 2nd Edition [online]. 2015. [Accessed 9 April 2015]. Available from: http://www.birmingham.ac.uk/Documents/libraries/9674-library-skills-student-ext-2-aw-web.pdf

[26] University of Birmingham *Visiting our libraries* [online]. 2015. [Accessed 9 April 2015]. Available from: http://www.birmingham.ac.uk/libraries/fesupport/visits.aspx

[27] Sixth Form student (name omitted for confidentiality purposes). Conversation. March 2015

Case Study 8

Cloud Computing: Using Google Apps

Darren Flynn, Andrew Walls and Caroline Shaw
The Bridge Learning Commons, Dixons Allerton Academy, Bradford
Winner of the SLA Inspiration Award (secondary category) 2014

Situation

One of the responsibilities of the Learning Commons at Dixons Allerton Academy is to investigate and implement innovative and effective uses of technology in the school setting. In addition to this there was a drive towards a learning model that operated on a 24/7 basis and facilitated greater collaboration between learners. One key area that the team has been looking into is the rollout and use of cloud computing in order to improve the educational experience of our students, in particular Post-16 students.

The rationale behind our drive towards cloud computing has been twofold; a practical consideration of the needs and limitations of a traditional networked environment; and a pedagogical assessment looking at how cloud computing can increase student engagement and achievement.

Practical Considerations

Within the Learning Commons we manage a wide variety of devices to support students' independent learning, including laptops, PCs and tablet computers. The key problem the team observed was the slow login time students experienced, which could range from a few seconds to 5–10 minutes, resulting in real and significant barriers to learning. In lessons teachers might struggle to plan activities effectively as students were able to get onto their network areas at significantly different speeds and during study periods the time lag between borrowing a device and being able to begin working led to poor study habits and distractions. On investigation with the IT team we found the main cause was the large amount of traffic going through the network. Cloud computing offered a solution as all files could be stored and accessed remotely, as needed, without being downloaded through the network, and programs such as word processing packages could be used through a browser window rather than being loaded onto network areas.

Pedagogy

An even more convincing argument for the team was the potential educational benefits cloud computing would offer the academy. Cloud documents would allow teachers to view and feedback on student work at any time without a reliance on hand-in dates or printed work. Students could view, act on and reply to feedback, creating a far richer feedback dialogue with teachers. Sharing files created via cloud computing would also facilitate new ways of working and collaboration between students. Documents could be edited by multiple contributors in real-time and shared between students and teachers instantly.

Finally, sharing permissions allows third-parties instant, remote and unmediated access to student work for review, feedback and delivery of information. For example, information literacy interventions could take place beyond traditional IL sessions and feedback could be given on the work itself. In practice this has meant that guidance and feedback could be given by subject experts to students, despite the limitations of constrained contact hours.

Action

On appointment of an e-learning specialist within the Learning Commons team, the cloud computing agenda gathered pace. Google Apps for Education (GAFE) was selected because the service was free and was used by a number of innovative schools and educators already. The school signed up for GAFE and accounts were created for all staff and students. GAFE was initially trialled with a number of different stakeholders to evaluate the service and develop best practice.

Teaching in a Cloud Environment

The Learning Commons team used GAFE exclusively with a Post-16, Level 2 Project Qualification group, replacing all course materials and workbooks with Google Docs. Students completing the qualification did all work using Google Apps and all written feedback was given on the platform. This action showed that GAFE could effectively replace traditional word processing programs and eliminated the need for printed documents, that teacher feedback/marking and student responses could be improved by using cloud technology, and that students could easily use the platform with training and modelling. An additional benefit was discovered by the team in terms of work monitoring: the teaching team could see when and how much work was completed in any given period. This data painted a rich picture for the team on how students were progressing in their work. Rather than being reliant on assessing and feeding back on work through periodic hand-in dates (where students worked in a vacuum), the team

could dip in and out of their work, give frequent formative feedback and identify and rectify issues early. This allowed for far greater pastoral and academic support of students undertaking the qualification.

The platform was also trialled during stand-alone projects, and interventions delivered collaboratively with teachers and with us, the Learning Commons team. We have a practice of joint-planned and delivered projects with teaching staff and, in the planning of these, GAFE was promoted as a tool for in-class and home working, for both individual and group assignments. The use of GAFE platforms was developed with the specific learning objectives identified in consultation with teaching staff. These projects demonstrated that teachers and students were both confident with, and could see the benefit of, cloud working. They also showed that teachers and the Learning Commons team could better monitor and feedback on student work with greater depth and regularity.

Constant experimentation of different teaching techniques and activities has allowed us to build up a body of experience of how cloud technology is best deployed in a variety of learning environments. This knowledge has been shared with our teaching colleagues through direct teaching interventions, in-class support, modelling and co-planning lessons and schemes of work. The team have shown how different Google Apps can be used in order to improve both the teaching of curriculum content and delivery of 'soft-skills', such as communication and collaboration between students.

Google Docs

Google's word-processing software in essence works similarly to most word-processing packages, the key difference being the ability of multiple users to work simultaneously on a single document in real-time and to share these documents easily. On a basic level, Docs has allowed staff and students to access documents on multiple devices. Staff can also use the comments feature for paperless feedback and to see that feedback is acted on and resolved. Higher-order usage allows for collaborative tasks such as collective note-taking, joint-authored work and sharing learning materials between different staff and students. As individual contributions are tracked, students have greater accountability for their efforts in any collaborative or group assignment, while the teacher can identify individual strengths and weaknesses within a piece of group work. Differing access permissions also allows for access beyond the teacher and student for specialised feedback from third-parties (such as our information literacy input) or for quality assurance and internal invigilation.

Examples of Use

Google Sheets

GAFE's spreadsheet software enables learning activities far beyond traditional spreadsheet packages. Again, simultaneous access and editing allows students to share knowledge and findings instantly. This has particular applications in subjects such as science; students might record the results of an individual or group experiment on a joint spreadsheet, allowing them to draw conclusions based on the results of numerous experiments (modelling on a classroom scale the real-life dissemination of scientific knowledge).

Google Slides

Slides allows students to create presentations. At a basic level this acts as a substitution of other slideshow software with the benefit of increased access for creation and viewing on multiple devices and to facilitate collaborative creation. For staff, easy sharing of slideshows removes the need for email or shared-areas, and differing editing permissions enables students to view while colleagues may edit. Comment features allow students to comment on, question or seek clarification on the slideshow's content directly. In higher-order use, Slides can be used for collaborative learning; the teacher might include an image, video or text on the slide and invite students to comment on its content. Taken further, students could respond to or expand upon others' contributions. The final product represents the thoughts, feelings and knowledge of the group as a whole.

Google Forms

GAFE's survey software allows for the simple collection and collation of student voice. In teaching, Forms can be used for quizzes, as a pre-assessment tool to inform differentiation, or for assessment for learning. As submissions are collated onto a single Google Sheet, responses can be easily shared with either colleagues or with students themselves. Forms can again be used to enable collaborative learning, drawing upon the knowledge, skills and experience of a whole class. One example of this use has been in information literacy instruction: students were given an essay question and asked to identify potential keywords for a literature search on a Form. Discussion prompted the development of further keywords and synonyms which were again submitted on the same form. This process was completed several times, each concentrating on a different aspect of the original question. All submissions were collated on a spreadsheet which was shared with all students. The result was a large list of potential keywords developed from the question, with many more than any single student could generate independently. This could be used as a reference tool when performing searches.

Google Drive

As a file storage system Drive shares many of the benefits of individual apps; increased and fast access (by student and teacher) to files, multiple-device support and (in the case of GAFE subscribers) unlimited storage. This decreases dependence on inefficient file storage and sending systems such as email, shared areas or virtual private networks. Simple file storage and archiving allows students access to past learning materials for revision or access to material such as presentations in advance of lessons to facilitate flipped-classroom methodology.

Google Classroom

The emerging use of Google Classroom, Google's blended learning platform, is showing huge potential for enhancing teaching and learning in the academy and making teachers' management of their multiple classes more streamlined and simple. Teachers can manage the workflows associated with multiple classes with far greater ease, setting class and home learning assignments electronically. Learning material is shared with all students through simple uploads and assignments. Electronic hand-ins allow for simple monitoring of work submissions (showing clearly who has or hasn't submitted work) and eliminates issues such as student absence on hand-in dates. For students, a whole year's work is available to view in a single place for exam revision or coursework.

GAFE, Student Experience and Initial Roll-Out

Student voice from Post-16 students had demonstrated dissatisfaction with the speed and login times on traditionally-networked devices during study periods. During investment in new and more devices, the team took the decision to keep these devices off the school domain: they would allow internet access but not access to files saved on the network. This greatly increased the speed and reliability of the devices but would require students to upload and convert their work to GAFE with Learning Commons staff providing support and training to facilitate this. The system envisioned was a blended environment; Post-16 students would work on a GAFE format during study periods on fast-access devices while retaining their network areas for in-class work. In practice, while many students embraced the change, this system was shown to be unsuitable for the needs of many students. Some were confused by having work in two different file formats, were unsure which device they should use for which task and had problems with additional services such as printing. At the end of an evaluative period the team had to end this trial and put the new laptops onto the network (with the associated issues of slowness and errors). The trial showed that while most students were willing and able to use cloud computing and appreciated the benefits, a hybrid environment of network access with additional cloud services was not an adequate solution.

The Learning Commons team consulted with SLT, e-safety group, IT support, Post-16 and Learning and Teaching teams to propose a one-to-one rollout where all Post-16 students would receive a personal Chromebook. A number of benefits were highlighted; increased access to IT resources (within the Post-16 cohort and the wider school, via timetabling Post-16 lessons out of IT suites), faster and more reliable internet access and learning and teaching benefits. The proposal was accepted and the Learning Commons team led on the scheme. A due-diligence exercise and report highlighted the future actions necessary to make the rollout successful and avoid the unforeseen negative consequences of many one-to-one schemes many other UK schools have experienced. The e-learning specialist and members of SLT visited leading Google Apps schools to see first-hand innovative and effective uses of cloud technologies in teaching and learning.

A key prerequisite of a successful GAFE rollout was identified as staff confidence, experience, and ideas for using cloud technology in teaching. Again the Learning Commons team took a leadership role in delivering staff CPD on GAFE to all Post-16 teachers. Staff were further supported by the Learning Commons team by sharing existing best practice amongst staff and through informal, ad hoc support. Staff buy-in and confidence in using GAFE for teaching and learning has grown and a number of individuals and departments have developed creative applications of the technology.

Result

The result of our promotion of cloud computing has been an exponential growth of its use in the academy. GAFE use has increasingly become the default position within Post-16 teaching and learning and is filtering down into other year groups. Post-16 students now use GAFE almost exclusively for school and home learning. The benefits of cloud computing are being seen in feedback, student work monitoring and collaborative approaches. Classroom usage has greatly enhanced the potential applications for the use of technology in teaching and learning. GAFE has significantly contributed to the ambition to create a genuine 24/7 learning culture in the academy.

Furthermore the multi-disciplinary make-up of the Learning Commons team has ensured that the move towards cloud computing is part of a 'joined-up' approach in other areas; GAFE has been integrated into both the academy's VLE strategy and a large-scale investment in a Post-16 e-library. The team has built a reputation as leaders in innovative, experienced and experimental teaching and learning practitioners.

Contributors

Lucy Atherton BA (Hons), MA, MCLIP, is currently Head Librarian at Wellington College, Berkshire. She has worked in a variety of libraries including the BBC, school libraries in Italy and Brazil and public libraries in Kent and Medway. She thoroughly enjoys her dual role of inspiring young people to read for pleasure and helping them develop information and digital literacy skills. She is particularly interested in finding new ways to engage students with digital sources and libraries through the use of games and interactive workshops.

Rosalind Buckland MCLIP, BA (Hons) Information & Library Management, worked in county and university libraries before moving to the secondary school sector and considers herself fortunate to be in a job that involves working with books and young people, a winning combination! She is currently employed in one of Lancashire's most oversubscribed schools, a non-selective co-ed Academy that she is proud to describe as a 'reading' school, where she delivers timetabled Library and Reading lessons. Rosalind is currently Chair of SLA Lancashire branch, a committee member on the SLA National Executive, and also CILIP's School Libraries Group.

James Curtis BA (Hons), MA, has been the Librarian of Holland Park School since 2012, when he joined to establish library provision in a whole school rebuild. Before joining Holland Park he completed his MA in Library and Information Studies at University College London, gaining experience of working in institutional libraries such as the RIBA collections and the V&A. Always passionate about books and reading, he has a firm belief that there is a book or author for every student.

Sally Dring MA (Hons), MCLIP, is currently the Learning Resources Manager at Ripon Grammar School where she has been for six years. Prior to that, she worked for nine years at The Hayfield School in Doncaster. She was a late-comer to library work, beginning from scratch at the age of 40, completing a City & Guilds Library and Information Assistants qualification, followed by an NVQ Level 3 in Information and Library Services. She finally Chartered through CILIP in 2011. Sally was a founding member of the Yorkshire and Humberside branch of the School Library Association in 2004 and has been Chair of the branch since then. She is currently an elected member of the SLA Executive Board, working with the Publications Committee. A more recent involvement is as a CILIP Mentor for Chartership, which she is thoroughly enjoying. At Ripon Grammar School she has been Literacy and Numeracy Co-ordinator for three years and particularly enjoys trying to build reading for pleasure and literacy strategies into all the different subject areas.

Following a graduate traineeship at a school Library in Bristol, and studying for her Masters degree in Birmingham, **Helen Emery** has 13 years' experience running the LRC at King Edward VI School, Lichfield. For the past three years she has also had a whole school responsibility for Literacy Across the Curriculum. Helen was highly commended in the SLYA 2011 and am SLA Staffordshire Branch Chair. She is passionate about equipping our students with skills for life through information literacy and reading for pleasure.

Darren Flynn is currently Information Literacy Lead at The Bridge Learning Commons at Dixons Allerton Academy, a large all-through academy in West Yorkshire. He is responsible for integrating information and digital literacy and academic skills into the curriculum alongside directly teaching project groups in Key Stage 3 and the EPQ in school. Darren is passionate about the opportunities that changes in technology, society and education offer to improve library and information services. He shares his experiences and learning widely through working closely with librarians in other institutions and through professional associations.